TeachingHorse

Rediscovering Leadership

By June Gunter, Ed.D.
Photographs by Beth A. Hyjek, MFA

AuthorHouse™
1663 Liberty Drive, Suite 200
Bloomington, IN 47403
www.authorhouse.com
Phone: 1-800-839-8640

© 2007 June Gunter, Ed.D.. All rights reserved.

No part of this book may be reproduced, stored in a retrieval system, or transmitted by any means without the written permission of the author.

First published by AuthorHouse   9/10/2007

ISBN: 978-1-4343-3605-7 (sc)

Library of Congress Control Number: 2007906679

Printed in the United States of America
Bloomington, Indiana

This book is printed on acid-free paper.

Cover Illustration by Patrick Pauluzzi
www.artworkbypatrick.com

Dedication

For My Teachers…
Yani,
Rocky,
Harley,
Dream,
Hope,
Lucky,
Galen, and
Grace.

Table of Contents

Dedication iii
Acknowledgements vii
Preface ix
Introduction 1
MareWisdom 11
MareWisdom in Action 13
Attention 16
Direction 21
Energy 27
Congruence 34
Community 40
Grace 49
The Way Closing 56
Conclusion: Horse Sense 61
Epilogue 65
Bibliography 71
About the Author 73
About the Photographer 73

Acknowledgements

In 1991, my life was struck by a bolt of clarity. Time stood still the day I met Beth Hyjek. I had no idea where life would take me, but I knew I would be making the journey with her. Beth has been beside me through every step, every fall, every disappointment, every loss, every shovel full of manure, and every triumph along the way.

I cannot write another word without thanking my parents, the late Josef Karl and Betty M. Gunter, for preparing me to live in this world without them. Both of them knew that I would never allow myself to be truly guided by another human being other than them. I am quite sure this is why mother inspired me to listen to horses.

My sister, Reverend Laura Early, happens to be cut from the same cloth. I am grateful for her presence in my life, her unflinching faith in me, her gentle reminders to remember who I am when I forget, and her company in our shared extraordinary adventure with horses.

My thanks also go to Barbara ("B") Pollard, Beth's mother, who has taken me in as one of her own and been there for both of us when we needed it most.

Ariana Strozzi taught me the craft of equine-guided education. Most importantly, Ariana taught me how to honor the horse as a guide. I am forever honored to call myself her student, her friend, and a member of her herd. I also want to give special acknowledgement to JetStar, a member of Ariana's herd, who was my first and life-altering Strozzi Ranch teacher.

Ariana gave me a second extraordinary gift when she introduced me to Barbara K. Rector. In this field of equine-guided education, you are never more than six degrees of separation from Miss Barbara. She is the fairy godmother of our work.

Alyssa Aubrey and I have walked the path of learning to be equine-guided educators together. I am so thankful to have had someone with whom to share the challenges, small wins, and big breakthroughs that have occurred along our simultaneous journeys. I can always count on Alyssa to remind me that I am not crazy and I am not alone.

Neda DeMayo, founder of the Return to Freedom Wild Horse Sanctuary, is the embodiment of the term horsewoman. Neda's commitment to be an advocate on behalf of the American wild horse is unwavering. I am forever indebted to Neda for entrusting Beth and I with the care of three horses from the sanctuary, Lucky, Hope, and Dream.

Carolyn Resnick taught me the language of horses. My horses breathed sighs of relief on the day I opened her book, and my world with horses was transformed from the moment I stood in her presence.

Many thanks go out to all of the friends of *TeachingHorse* who had the courage to move into unknown territory with us, and who gave us their unfailing encouragement to stay on the path when our doubts were the heaviest. Betty and Tony Adams, Ann Alden, Kehau Aspen, Terri Aspen, CJ Blaney, Peter Block, Terry Bream, Cortney and Gary Buckmaster, Jami Butler, Anna Calek, Tim and Sharon Clapp, Anne Cloe, Guy Chicoine, Vickie Cottle, Michele Crumes, Beth Dixson, Kelly Dixon Furr, Lynn Dixson, Judy Dolmatch, Bill Early, Gunter Early, June Michele Early, Vicki Enriquez, Faith Evans, Gaby Fabian, Katie and Cully Fredricksen, Sandy Forsyth, Gloria Gilford-Logan, Brenda Graf, Judy Hilyard, Sarah Healy, Sara Hopkins-Powell, Katie Hyjek, Jodi Joyce, Karen Kaufman, Sherry Keen, Sandy Kobrock, Deanna Konrath, Steve Lillie, Sharon Medhi, Debra Mipos, Rosann Moulis, Julie Nelson, Ronnie Noize, Tony Oakley, Mike O'Neill, Susie Orton, Toula Ousouljoglou, Mari Parino, Mary Piper, Wayne Philippi, Richard Pitts, Debi Sanks, Linda Brown Schaeff, Jill Steinbruegge, Maggie Shreve, John Tarrant, Kati Traunweiser, Lisa Wall, and Lib Widmer.

The eight horses from **Grace Mountain Ranch** have been central to the work of *TeachingHorse*. Many other horses across the country have also both touched our lives and taught us profound lessons. Their names are as follows. From **Strozzi Ranch**: Lacy, JetStar, Ruby, Lottie, Superman, Sunny, Stella, Lightning, Tess, Cowgirl, Sadie, Lilly, Jane, and Billy. From **Centerline Farms**: Ptarmingan, Mariachi, Strawberry, Ubu, Mooney, Merlin, Blackie, Fred, Nightcap, and Rock. From **Early Bird Stables**: Sunny, Twister, Penny Perfect, Ricochet, Annie, and Blessing. From **Discovering Equus**: Lucky, Sokki, Generator, Dixie, and Shadow. From **Adventures in Awareness**: Crackers, Serra June, Buckingham, Sum Punk, and Sip Ahoy.

Preface

"There are no paved roads when you are on your own path. They are all just dirt." – Quentin Tarantino

In a herd of horses, leadership is shared. The lead mare sets the direction and pace of the herd. The lead stallion keeps the herd together and protects it from predators. Each member of the herd has a role in protecting the health of the herd. One horse is often recognized for its ability to notice the presence of a potential predator and is referred to as the sentinel or ambassador of the herd. This horse will be the first line of defense, advancing toward potential threats to assess if they are friend or foe and taking decisive action. All of the horses in the herd contribute to the socialization of new or young members, teaching them what behaviors are acceptable and reprimanding those who behave in ways that could compromise the health of the herd. The ever-present goal of herd leadership is health, harmony, and unity.

Health, harmony, and unity: what a fresh way to think about leadership. Our world needs a new way to think about leading that will result in creating healthy, sustainable communities. We could not ask for better teachers than horses, because creating thriving communities is what herds of horses have been able to accomplish for millions of years.

This book is a chronicle of my journey toward discovering what horses have to teach us about leadership and living in a community. I have spent many years studying herd dynamics and the language of horses, and yet the most valuable lessons I have learned have come from living in a community with my herd of horses. My journey was initiated by my lead mare, Yani. Our life together inspired the formulation of a model of leadership based on how lead mares lead their herds. I refer to the model of leadership as "MareWisdom."

The book begins with the story of how I was introduced to horses as teachers. The next two chapters describe the MareWisdom model of leadership and give a detailed account of what MareWisdom looks like in action. The next four chapters describe each of the four components of the model of leadership and give examples of how leaders have worked with horses to improve their skills with an innovative approach to learning known as equine-guided education. The last three chapters delve deeper into what horses have to teach us about living in a community. The book ends with a conclusion that brings my story full circle and serves as a call to action to answer a fundamental question. What will your community learn about leadership from you?

In the stories that are told, I frequently refer to people by first name only to protect their privacy. Depending on the person's wishes, some of the names have been changed to protect confidentiality. All of the horses' names you will read are accurate. I hope you enjoy getting to know each and every one of these extraordinary teachers.

Introduction
"Listen, listen, listen. Allow, allow, allow." – Barbara K. Rector

I had just pulled into the driveway of my new house in Walnut Creek, California when I noticed an old yellow tabby tomcat lounging in the planter on the front porch. He reminded me of a cat named O'Malley I had as child. I had only lived in this new house for a few days and had never seen him before. Being the cat person that I am, I introduced myself. Taking the loving blink of his eyes as an invitation, I picked him up and began petting him. As we were enjoying each other's company, my neighbor drove up and pulled in her driveway. The old tomcat let me know it was time for him to go. He trotted across the street to see my neighbor. The next day when I came home from work, there he was again, sunning himself in the planter. I saw my neighbor's car in the driveway and decided to check to see if this magnificent old cat was hers.

With the cat in my arms I headed across the street. I rang the doorbell and a woman who was about to change my life forever answered the door. I said, "Hi. I'm your new neighbor. Is this your cat?"

She looked sheepishly at me and said, "Yes, his name is Tiger and he loves to lie in your planter. I know he is thin. He is very old and is in renal failure."

I interrupted her by saying, "Please don't worry. I am a cat lover and just wanted to make sure he had a home. My name is June."

She replied, "Hi, I'm Rosann."

The conversation then took a serendipitous turn. I said, "Hey, I see you have a horse trailer. Do you have a horse that goes with it?"

She laughed and said, "I do. I board him at a barn a couple of miles away."

I then told her that I was looking to buy a horse. She let me know that the barn owner had a few for sale that I could look at sometime.

Rosann was a bit taken aback when I showed up the very next day. I arrived at the barn to find her brushing her horse and getting ready to ride. She stopped what she was doing and began to point out the horses that were for sale. Among them was a little buckskin quarter horse mare whose presence captivated me from the moment I saw her. I made a beeline for her, and the entire world disappeared.

Rosann's voice began to sound like someone talking when you have earplugs in your ears. I put my hand on that gorgeous mare's neck and turned to Rosann and said, "This is the one I want. How much is she and whom do I pay?"

In complete shock and disbelief, Rosann said, "Don't you want to look at the other horses and at least ride her first?"

"Nope. She's the one, and I would love to ride her! What is her name?"

With her head still tilted in disbelief, Rosann said, "Her name is Yani." It was a moment I will never forget as long as I live.

On the outside, you would have thought my life could not have been better. Nothing could have been further from the truth. At the time, I was in a leadership position where I felt stuck and devalued. I was staying in the job purely out of fear of losing my income. I was also dealing with the loss of both of my parents, two people I adored with all my heart. I had become someone I did not know and certainly did not like. When I felt myself drawn into Yani's eyes, it was as if my path back to myself had been set in motion through her, with the help of Tiger and my dear friend Rosann.

I had grown up riding horses, and in a flash of complete insanity, I decided I needed to get back to my roots. I bought Yani that day and had no idea what I had just done. Yani is a well-bred, highly sensitive, athletic cutting horse. The horses I grew up with were bomb-proof trail horses. I had just bought a horse that I did not have the skills to ride. Of course, I believed that I knew how to ride horses, even though I had not been riding for twenty years. So I took Yani out on a trail ride just a few days after I bought her, just the two of us. It wasn't long before Yani let me know in no uncertain terms that I had not earned her trust and was not in a position to lead her down an unknown trail. I learned several important lessons that day, the day of my "wake up fall." Sparing you most of the details, I'll simply say that Yani got scared and did not trust me to keep her safe. We both fell backwards down a hill. I wound up sliding neck-first under a barbed wire fence and ended up with a broken left wrist. Thankfully, Yani was okay and I had enough courage left in me to get up and ride her the two miles home.

Horses are flight animals who gain their safety from traveling in a herd. When they smell danger or feel unsafe, they turn around and run. I basically ignored Yani's nature when I asked her to go on that trail alone with me. She let me know that she did not trust me to protect her and that I had not earned a place in her herd. The saddest part was that I was expecting her to want to take care of me. I had reached a point in my life when I was tired of being in charge. I was living a fear-driven life. I had lost all confidence in myself and was in no frame of mind to lead anyone – and Yani knew it.

Yani expected me to be the leader, to set the direction, and to guide us on our journey. When we headed around the corner of the trail into unknown territory, she could sense that I was not paying attention to where we were going. Horses survive based on their ability to sense and respond to changes in energy in their environment. Yani obviously sensed danger down the road. It was a danger that I was unable to see or feel, because I wasn't looking and I was numb. Since that fall, I have worked diligently to earn Yani's and all of my horses' trust and confidence in me as leader. These horses have led me on a path of discovering a new way to think about leadership.

While I was recovering from my broken left wrist, Yani developed lameness in her left front hoof. We discovered she had navicular disease, a painful condition affecting a horse's hoof, which required her to be on "stall rest" and led to even more difficulties. She was filled with nervous energy and became dangerously unpredictable and very unhappy. I grew more fearful of Yani each day. There are no words to explain what it feels like to love a being so deeply and be excruciatingly afraid of her at the same time.

At this point in my career, I traveled a great deal. When I got home from a business trip, the first thing I wanted to do was to go spend time with Yani. However, the desire to spend time with Yani quickly morphed into a daunting sense of responsibility and a nauseating feeling that I was risking my life each time I opened her stall door. Because the horses I grew up with were very well trained, I had never learned how to manage a hard-to-handle horse. I didn't even recognize that I didn't know how to manage a difficult horse. I also didn't know where to turn. Just when I was about to give up on myself, the universe sent me Mari Parino.

Mari was a trainer at the barn where I kept Yani. She specialized in preparing horses to be a part of a handicapped riding program. Her specialty was teaching ground manners to horses and desensitizing them to objects that horses are typically afraid of encountering.

At our barn, Yani had developed quite a reputation. She could clear an arena full of other horses in no time flat, so we had the arena to ourselves a lot. Knowing full well the situation we were in, Mari agreed to work with Yani and me anyway. I am forever grateful for her courage and dedication.

Mari worked with Yani and me for several months, teaching both of us the basics of groundwork, leading in hand, and most importantly, how to earn each other's trust. We made great progress, and things were going pretty smoothly – until one afternoon. Out of nowhere, Yani had an unpredictable panic attack in the aisle of the barn. For no apparent reason she reared up, lost her balance, and fell over backwards. Thankfully Mari was there to witness the event. After Yani settled down and recovered, I asked Mari, "Did I do that?"

Mari replied shaking her head, "No, absolutely not, and we will probably never know what did."

Yani was my only horse at this point, and she was not safe to ride on the trails. I was at my wits end.

After the third time Yani had thrown me and several hospital bills later, I was trying to decide whether to consult another trainer. When five different people on a list of people in my life, none of which knew each other, recommended that I go see the same horseperson, I was pushed past my indecision. Again I was about to meet a woman who would change my life forever. Her name is Ariana Strozzi.

Ariana is an accomplished horsewoman and a pioneer in the field of equine-guided education. We began our relationship when I attended a workshop offered at Strozzi Ranch. It was one of those workshops where I learned a lot more about myself than I had intended to do that day. After hearing my stories about my bumpy relationship with Yani, my new mentor, Ariana, simply said, "Well, she obviously has a lot to teach you."

Ariana's belief is that horses can teach us about how we show up in the world and how to see the blind spots that keep us from realizing a vision. In one of the workshop activities, the goal was to form a partnership with a horse I had never ridden. The horse was not wearing a bridle, only a halter and lead rope. I had to lead the horse to go left or right without a bit and reins. It was like the first time I tried to ride a bike without holding onto the handlebars. I had to pay special attention to the signals I was sending through my balance, my breathing, and my line of sight. Eventually, the new horse and I started to work together, but it was not without awkwardness and struggle.

When I got off the horse, Ariana asked me, "How did it feel?"

I said, "I hated it! I just want to get back on my own horse. Even though she has thrown me, at least I know her."

Ariana replied, "So, is that showing up anywhere else in your life?"

And there I was, facing the mirror. I am the kind of person who enjoys the comfort of well established relationships with my family, friends, and long-standing clients. Networking and forming new relationships have always seemed exhausting to me. I was now in the process of starting a new life and a new business; therefore, I was dealing with all of the awkwardness of developing new business relationships and learning to work with new people. I know now that if I had not taken the time to look in the mirror with the help of horses, I would still be avoiding the work I needed to do to realize my dreams.

When I reached the point where I was not sure what to do with Yani, I asked Ariana if she would come and evaluate Yani, and give me her opinion on what my options were. Ariana drove into the barn as I was leading Yani from her stall into the turnout area. As soon as I slipped the halter off of Yani, she began galloping along the rail of the arena as fast as she could go, around and around. Finally she exhausted herself and came to a dead stop in front of where I was standing on the outside of the rail. Ariana said, "Well, she has two speeds – on and off."

What caught me so off guard was that was exactly the way my life felt. I would run full out at work during the week and completely collapse on the weekends. Ariana helped me understand that Yani was suffering from "over-containment." As I listened to Ariana, I thought, "Yeah that makes two of us."

Ariana then made an extraordinary offer to let Yani come and live with her at Strozzi Ranch. Yani would have a stall triple the normal size with her own private pasture, next to Ariana's herd. This opportunity would give us a chance to see if having a more natural life would take care of the symptoms of over-containment.

As generous as this offer was, the decision was agonizing for me. Ariana's ranch was about an hour and a half drive from my house. I would only be able to see Yani on the weekends. I remember sobbing as I dialed the number, calling Ariana to tell her that if the offer was still good, I would like to bring Yani to her ranch.

The next day, Yani was loaded on a trailer and we made the trip to her new home. I kid you not, something happened to Yani the minute she backed off that trailer and walked into her new pasture. It was like she exhaled and let out years worth of anxiety. I drove back to see her the next day, and I would have sworn Yani had been drinking fine red wine after a full body massage from a spa in Napa Valley. Yani was completely transformed into a relaxed and calm horse. I grew to understand that this state of contentment is what can happen when you let a horse be a horse.

After months of working with Yani in this setting without incident and many profound riding lessons with Ariana, I knew that Yani and I were going to be just fine. It was then I decided to leave California and find a home we could both enjoy. During a trip to work with my new business partners, I discovered southern Oregon. The land prices were still reasonable and it was definitely horse country. My partner Beth Hyjek and I were blessed to find a forty-five acre ranch complete with a house, new barn, and riding arena for less than the price of my house in California. We were about to begin a pivotal time in each of our lives in a magical place we named Grace Mountain Ranch.

As it turned out, my journey with Ariana extended far beyond my relationship with Yani and became about my relationship with humanity. In 2001, I began the process with Ariana of becoming an equine-guided educator. Equine-Guided Education (EGE) is the craft of providing learning experiences with the help and guidance of horses. I completed several years of training to prepare me to serve as a bridge between the horse and human worlds and to engage people in experiences with horses that result in profound growth in their personal and professional journeys.

In 2004, just a few months after we moved to Grace Mountain Ranch, Beth and I founded **TeachingHorse** as an organization and official provider of Equine-Guided Education. **The mission of TeachingHorse is to bring horses and humans together to inspire new ways of thinking about leadership and creating healthy, sustainable communities.**

Over the last six years, I have experienced hundreds of occasions where horses were able to release people from the paralyzing and unhealthy beliefs that were robbing them of their lives. I would be remiss if I did not introduce you to the original **TeachingHorse** faculty. Their names are Rocky, Harley, and of course, Yani. The week we arrived in Oregon, we added two horses to our family so that Yani would have a herd.

Rocky is an eighteen year old sorrel quarter horse-mix gelding standing 15.1 hands high. He has earned the distinction of being our healing horse. He is able to sense when people have visceral or emotional energetic blocks and give them very perceptive and clear information about what they need to be listening to in their hearts and bodies.

Harley is a sixteen year old buckskin quarter horse gelding standing 16.2 hands high. He is our often misunderstood, brave and steady giant who will test your commitment to being a leader and setting boundaries. Truth be told, Harley is Yani's guy. He diligently watches over her, and we adore him for it. Harley has also been a great teacher for learning the art of surrender. Most people believe you surrender to things you don't want. True surrender is to give yourself over to things you do want, like happiness and rest. I have written one poem in my entire life. It was inspired by and was for Harley.

Surrender to Life

Let your knees buckle,
Fall over,
Take a final look around.

Notice,
Exhale,
Let your cheek plummet to the ground.

Surrender to the joy of a nap,
In the afternoon sun.
Rest, full, perfect.

As for Yani, she has settled into her mare wisdom and has developed an extraordinary level of maternal patience for working with people who do not understand horses. Yani will gently guide you into rethinking everything you once thought to be true about what it means to be a leader. She will test the level at which you are paying attention and the clarity of your direction. Yani will then demand that you follow that direction with focused energy, and she will act as a revealing mirror regarding your level of congruence and authenticity. All the while, she gives you an overwhelming sense of unconditional love. In 2006, Yani gave birth to her first foal, our beloved Grace. Grace is a yearling red dun quarter horse/paint cross filly. Watching Yani raise Grace has been the ultimate lesson in leadership steeped in mare wisdom.

MareWisdom
"People and animals are supposed to be together." – Temple Grandin

In my journey with Yani, I have learned what it takes to earn the right to be the lead mare of a herd, based on watching Yani with her herd and observing the many other horses that have since touched my life. For herd members to place their trust in a lead mare, they must know four things about her. One, she is paying **attention** and can detect even the most subtle shifts in the environment. Two, she can give them clear **direction** on how to respond to the shifts. Three, she is able to follow that direction with focused **energy,** providing the herd with guidance on the pace (i.e., walk, trot, canter) with which to respond. Four, she displays **congruence** of her inner and outer expressions. Who she presents to them on the outside is the same as she is on the inside. Ultimately, the herd members must know that the lead mare has their best interest as her source of motivation at all times.

Attention, direction, energy, congruence: when a lead mare demonstrates these characteristics and skills, the herd becomes confident in her leadership. The bottom line is that confidence in the leader makes the herd agile in times of change.

The same is true for people. To gain our confidence, our leaders must demonstrate that they are paying attention to what is going on in their communities/organizations, are able to give clear direction with focused, inspiring energy, and are so authentic that their intentions can be fully trusted. Confidence in leadership makes a community or an organization agile when the time for change can no longer be avoided. Horses are the best teachers we could ask for when we want to learn the skills of agility in the midst of uncertainty and increase confidence in our leadership.

Al Gore recently published a book and produced a film entitled *An Inconvenient Truth*. The film describes the global warming trends affecting our environment and pleads for us to respond in ways that might make us uncomfortable or inconvenience our current way of life but will protect the survival of our world. Herein lies the difference between the human and horse worlds. For horses, there is no inconvenient truth – just truth, just reality. As human beings, we struggle to let go of the idea that being comfortable is the goal. Of course horses enjoy feeling comfortable and being in a routine. At the same time, they are not so attached to the feeling that they are willing to let their herd die to preserve it. When horses notice their environment changing, for instance, a fire on the horizon or a predator coming closer, they don't stand around and wish for the good ole days to return. Horses take action; they move, no matter how uncomfortable it makes them, with the lead mare out front guiding the way.

MareWisdom in Action

"Horses speak in silence, never forgetting to listen." – Carolyn Resnick

Recently we adopted three American wild horses from the Return to Freedom Wild Horse Sanctuary. Their names are Lucky, Dream, and Hope. They are brother and sisters of a herd originating from Hart Mountain, Oregon, and were sired by the same stallion. All three horses were born in 2001, so they are now six years old. In my studies of horses, I have read a great deal about herd dynamics, but there is nothing like observing them firsthand. My first day with these three amazing creatures was life-changing.

On a magnificent, clear spring Oregon morning, I watched the little herd move around its new pasture. It looked almost like a team of trick horses moving in synchronized motion. The sight caught me off guard, because my domesticated herd of three has never moved that way. Yani, Rocky, and Harley travel together, but they do not move together. This little wild herd moves like it is one body. Clearly, they are of one mind and one heart, even with their already detectable, adorable individual uniqueness and personalities.

Dream, a red roan with a long and flowing rich red mane, is the lead mare. This fact became apparent in the first few minutes of their arrival. When we led them from the trailer into their new home, Dream galloped the perimeter of the pasture as Lucky, her brother, and Hope, her sister, stayed close behind, following her every cue. You could immediately see her masterful ability to pay attention with her eyes and entire body. Dream was completely in the moment and she could see, hear, and feel with an intensity I can only imagine. Her direction was clear and her energy was focused. Hope and Lucky followed her without doubt or question. Their sense of confidence in her leadership was palpable.

Shortly afterward, Dream made her way to the fence line where my herd was waiting to greet the new arrivals. Dream went to greet Rocky, nose-to-nose. Their love at first sight was quickly interrupted by Lucky. Lucky ran in front of Dream and placed his full body between Rocky and the fence separating them from each other. It was almost as if he was saying, "Hey, that's my sister! Back off!" Dream graciously allowed her little brother's protection, but at the same time continued to stretch out her nose to Rocky. Their eyes never left each other. I was mesmerized.

It did not take long for me to sense that Rocky was meant to be the bridge between this little herd and its new life. Rocky has a grandfatherly way about him, a very clear sense of himself and nothing to prove.  Even though I knew there were risks involved, I opened the gate to let Rocky in the pasture. Dream and Rocky immediately and yet calmly walked up to each other and touched noses with beautifully arched necks. Their connected form created the shape of a heart. Lucky and Hope stood close by, waiting for Dream's next cue. Rocky made a 180 degree turn away from Dream and began walking into the pasture. If this scene had been photographed, the caption for Rocky would have read, "Come on pretty girl, I will show you around your new digs." Dream simply followed him as if they had known each other their entire lives. Lucky and Hope stayed close, but a bit behind, allowing Rocky and Dream their time to bond.

Later, with Rocky enraptured in spring grazing, Dream, Lucky, and Hope were off again to explore their pasture. When they looked across the way, they could see Yani and Harley in another pasture. As they approached the fence, another amazing thing happened. Lucky and Hope placed themselves on each side of Dream in an inverted "V" shape, blocking her from this potential threat. In an absolutely regal pose, Dream lifted her head and neck above them to get a closer look. There stood Yani, a mare pregnant in her tenth month, with Harley, her devoted gelding, at her side. The ladies nickered at each other, and both little herds relaxed completely and resumed grazing. All was well.

Upon further reflection, I still continue to be amazed at what horses have to teach us about leadership creating healthy, sustainable communities. As I watched Lucky and Hope move into protective stances for Dream, I found myself thinking, "How often do you hear about employees of organizations or members of communities stepping up to protect their leader in the face of a potential threat?" Most leaders are served up as scapegoats and lightning rods to absorb the storm (although these days some may well deserve such treatment). I can't tell you how many people I talk to who view leadership as a zero sum game that cannot be won. Therefore, they decide not to play. There have been times in my own life when I made the same choice. Be a leader? What for? No thanks. Lucky and Hope have mastered the art of accepting Dream's leadership, while not giving up their personal accountability and role in protecting the health of their herd. Dream has mastered the art of being able to both lead and follow, and honors the contribution of every member of the herd.

It has become clear to me that the way Yani and Dream view their roles as leaders is a refreshing departure from our society's current definition. Listen to some clichés about leadership. "It is lonely at the top." I can promise you that Yani and Dream are not lonely. "There is no rest for the weary." I watch Dream and Yani take glorious naps in the sun as the members of their herds watch over them with great care. I continue to be in awe of their mare wisdom. The question becomes, how can we bring MareWisdom into how we lead our organizations, communities, and families?

Attention

"It is important to notice when you fall into judgments that disconnect you from reality." – Linda Kohanov

In my work with communities and organizations, I find a commonality in the questions they are asking. What are the needs of the communities we serve? How are the needs of our customers changing? What will motivate our people to get engaged in achieving the vision of the organization? To answer these questions, leaders need to be paying attention.

Think of the number of times you have driven home from work and when you got home, you couldn't remember how you got there. You were on automatic pilot, not paying attention.

According to Jon Kabat-Zinn, as a society, we live in a state of continuous partial attention. In his book *Coming to Our Senses*, he tells a story of a father being thrilled with the fact that his "Blackberry" has given him the freedom to go to his son's baseball game, because he can now work at the same time. Neither his son nor his work is getting his full attention. I can tell you from personal experience that you cannot safely work with horses if you are on auto-pilot or giving them partial attention.

I learned from Carolyn Resnick, creator of the Liberty Method of equine training, that horses test your leadership skills by determining how well you are paying attention. Carolyn spent years living among and observing a natural herd of wild horses in the desert of southern California. She was able to observe how horses establish their pecking order and how they move up the hierarchy. One of the ways a horse gains status is by being able to catch another horse above it in the pecking order off guard or not paying attention. Their tests are very subtle. A horse will walk up behind another horse grazing and see how close it can get before the other horse notices. If the horse can get close enough to nip the other, it will. In that moment, a change in status takes place.

The lead mare demands that every herd member keeps an eye on her at all times and knows where she is. When she notices that she does not have a herd member's attention, she will abruptly and with swift clarity remind them of that rule of being a member of her herd. Carolyn summed it up best when she said, "When you are in the presence of a horse, she deserves your full attention."

One of the members of my herd, Harley, has been my best teacher for learning how to pay attention. At first I thought Harley came to us with some bad behaviors and was just being rude and pushy. I grew to understand that his behavior was a test. Harley, communicating in the language of horses, was saying, "Are you leading and protecting this herd? Because if you are not, I will."

Not all horses have the same intense, often perceived as aggressive, behavior that stallions or dominant geldings like Harley have. Harley believes it is his job to protect the herd, and he does this by testing whether or not you are paying attention. To earn the right to lead his herd, I have to demonstrate that I am paying attention and that he can count on me to keep him safe when we are together. I take great honor in the trust that he places in me. I am also very thankful for him, because I know that no harm will come to Yani and her new baby, Grace, while Harley is around.

Horses are profound teachers for remembering to notice what _is_ happening in your life rather than what you _think_ is happening. As Harley was teaching me the true art of paying attention, my ability to notice shifts in my environment, whether I was at work or in a pasture, grew exponentially. Learning to pay attention to reality has also become a focal point of our work with our clients.

Faith, one of our TeachingHorse clients, had an old fear of horses she wanted to overcome. She knew that old fears like this one were in the way of her creating healthy relationships in her life. When she heard about the work we were doing, she saw it as an opportunity to move beyond these fears in an interesting and safe way. Her first experience was a grooming exercise with Rocky. Here we began the process of decoding the language of horses in a way that gave Faith an increasing sense of self-control in how she related to them. While Faith was grooming Rocky, he stood completely still for a good thirty minutes. As she became comfortable enough to put her hands on his neck, her tears started to flow within seconds. Faith's tears and Rocky's compassionate presence were the beginning of washing away her fears. Faith was learning how to pay attention to her relationship with Rocky instead of her over-generalized fear of horses.

As Faith's confidence grew, she moved into more active groundwork exercises in the round pen with Yani. Her goal was to embody the clarity of direction and level of energy with which she wanted to live her life. The exercise involved getting Yani to move in a circle around Faith without the use of a halter or lead line. Yani's patience and forgiving nature were both touching and inspiring. After several awkward attempts, Faith was able to get and keep Yani moving with just her energy. She was able to experience in her body what she wanted her life to look and feel like in the future.

Even so, Faith was still doubtful that the horses were actually connecting to her. Faith had been working with Yani and Harley when we started to wrap up on the second day. At this point, we all received another lesson in paying attention. Rocky was grazing in the pasture when, for some unknown reason, he walked from the pasture into the center of the round pen. I thought he might be feeling left out, so I asked Beth to go see him. She gave him some attention and a treat, and then walked out. Rocky went back to the center of the round pen and just stood there. That was strange, so I went in. I spent some time with him and gave him a lot of appreciation, and then I walked out. He went right back to the center of the round pen, stood there, and looked at Faith. I said, "Faith, I think Rocky has something for you."

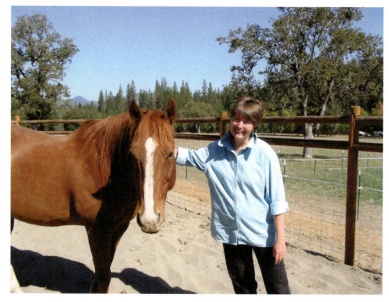

Faith walked over and stood at the entrance to the round pen. As soon as she walked in, Rocky stood beside her, shoulder-to-shoulder. Faith said to Rocky, "Will you walk with me?" They walked off together like they were soul mates. It was beautiful. Faith was radiant. Afterwards she turned to me and said, "Wow, so that is what partnership feels like, and all I had to do was ask." In that moment with Faith, we all experienced what happens when we pay attention to the opportunities presented to us and trust that when the student is ready, the teacher appears.

There are some important questions you can begin asking yourself on your journey of remembering how to pay attention.

- What do you truly care about?
- When do you feel joy?
- What is happening in your life right now?
- What do your loved ones see when they look at you?
- What has your body been trying to tell you?

As you reflect on these questions, if any of your answers are "I don't know," you have gotten an affirmation that regaining your ability to pay attention is critical for you.

Learning the art of paying attention to reality can be very freeing. Temple Grandin, author of *Animals in Translation*, summed it up nicely when she said, "Animals see what is there, we see what we think is there." What we fear is always worse than reality.

Recently I was teaching a leadership workshop for physicians and nurses and wound up in a conversation that is a disturbing testament to the state of our healthcare system. A nurse raised her hand and proceeded to tell me that she was about to enter the hospital for a procedure. She was afraid of what might happen to her while there, because of the common occurrence of medical errors. She had told her husband that he needed to stay with her around the clock. She asked me, "Should I tell my husband to be afraid and on alert?"

I sat down beside her to make sure she knew I was with her and I said, "Don't tell your husband to be afraid. Tell your husband to pay attention."

We have a lot to learn from horses in this area. Horses are prey animals. They live each day knowing that at any second a cougar could jump out of the woods and try to eat them. So how is it that they can enjoy a relaxed afternoon of grazing in a pasture? Horses have learned how to embody a state referred to as "relaxed and ready." They can be relaxed and grazing at one moment and moving away at a full gallop in the next. Even though they are relaxed, they are aware and are paying attention with their eyes and their entire bodies, keeping themselves agile and ready.

As an aside, being relaxed and ready is also a mantra for how to ride a horse. You learn to be relaxed in the saddle and ready for any moment at the same time. The way you respond to the unexpected is to relax even more with a heightened sense of awareness, giving the horse clear direction and confidence that you will lead them through the situation. Like leaders, riders who tense up and become rigid will lose the horse's confidence, and usually fall off. I learned that the hard way. We will be less paralyzed by fear when we learn to be relaxed and ready for the ride of our lives.

Direction

"We don't find confidence. Confidence finds us. Confidence arises out of a deep-seated belief in ourselves and what we care about." – Ariana Strozzi

Re-learning how to pay attention is a critical first step in creating confidence in your leadership. Next you must be able to give clear direction in response to reality as you see it. In an Equine-Guided Education workshop, one exercise is to learn how to longe a horse. In this activity, you ask the horse to move around you in a large circle with the horse wearing a halter attached to a thirty ft. lead line. The lead line symbolizes your connection and relationship to the horse.

In this exercise, it is not uncommon for participants to walk backwards while they are asking the horse to walk forward. When the person walks backwards, the horse simply follows them or sometimes just stops, waiting for clear direction. The person looks confused and does not understand why the horse will not walk forward. I will say, "Notice that you are walking backwards and asking the horse to walk forward at the same time."

Without fail, the participant will say, "No I am not!"

Invariably, one of the other participants will say, "Yeah, you were; I saw it, too."

The crowning teachable moment for the participant lies in my next question, "Is this happening anywhere else in your life?" Metaphorically speaking, think of the number of times you have set a new direction in your life, but you find yourself falling into old patterns of behavior and back into your comfort zone. In order to move forward, you must step forward.

In a recent TeachingHorse workshop, one of the participants, Sharon, was in the middle of starting a new business and was dealing with a great deal of frustration. In my experience with equine-guided education, who you are and what is happening in your life show up very quickly while working with the horses. Sharon began her turn at the exercise with Rocky. The best way for me to describe what I saw was that it looked like she was running in place, working very hard, and not getting any movement from Rocky. I said to Sharon, "It looks to me like you are running in place."

Sharon replied with exasperation, "That is what my life feels like right now!" She went on to explain that her new business was not making progress fast enough for her satisfaction.

Coaching her, I asked her to take a deep breath and center herself. "To become centered, take a deep breath in through your nose and exhale through your mouth. Stay present to your breath until you can feel your feet planted firmly on the ground. Clear your mind of all distractions and increase your awareness of what is happening in the moment. Bring clarity to your intention by focusing on what matters most to you in your life."

With her now both emotionally and intellectually quiet, I asked her what taking a step forward in this new direction would look like for her. Sharon quickly concluded that she was using old strategies that worked in her previous business, but were not going to work in this new one. It was time for her to think differently, if she was going to make this new business work. She decided what her next step should be based on new thinking. Seeing that she had this clarity in mind, I asked her to take that first step forward with Rocky. Rocky could sense her confidence and commitment, and they moved forward together with purpose and passion. Sharon was back on track and ready to fully embody the direction of her new business.

I have been amazed by the willingness of so many people to tap into the wisdom of horses to gain clarity on the direction of their lives. I am not really sure what prepared me to take direction from a horse, which is exactly what we mean when we use the term equine-guided education. Thankfully when Elisabeth came to visit us, I was ready to embrace the unexpected. Elisabeth scheduled a coaching session to help her gain some clarity on what was next for her in her life. She had been a member of a dance company whose production was ending. As she drove up the driveway of our ranch, Rocky saw the strange car and began to make his way to the gate. Somehow Rocky always knows when it is time for him to go to work.

Elisabeth stepped out of her car and was immediately drawn to Rocky. I shook her hand and walked with her over to the pasture gate where he was standing. Elisabeth held out her hand, with the greatest respect, for Rocky to give it a sniff. As soon as she did, Rocky turned around and went back out into the pasture and began grazing as if no one was there. I was completely surprised at his behavior; he had never done that before. I stood there quiet and in shock for a few seconds. Just as I was about to speak, Yani came up to the gate, stretched out her nose, tilted her head slightly down, and with her unmistakable, unconditionally loving eye looked right at Elisabeth.

I simply said, "Well Elisabeth, this is Yani. It seems as if Rocky and Yani have decided that she will be the best teacher for you today. How do you feel about that?"

Elisabeth said, "Cool."

The direction from Yani and Rocky to me was blazingly clear, although I had no idea at this point why they had made the switch between them. But in honoring these horses as guides, I did not need to know why. I trusted their direction.

Knowing that Elisabeth was here because she wanted to figure out what was next for her, I asked her a question, "What do you want your life to look and feel like from this point forward?"

Elisabeth replied, "I want to live large and loud in New York City!"

I responded in kind, "Cool. Let's bring Yani into this conversation."

The three of us went into the round pen. I explained and demonstrated the safety guidelines for working with horses at liberty in a round pen. Then I showed her how to get Yani moving around her in a circle by giving Yani clear direction with focused energy. Elisabeth watched every move I made as if a choreographer was teaching her a new dance. Now it was Elisabeth's turn. My final instruction to her was, "Show Yani what you want your life in New York to look and feel like. Show Yani large and loud."

Elisabeth's first attempt was anything but large and loud. It was more like forced and stiff to the music of her inner critic. After she struggled a bit to get Yani moving, I asked her to tell me what she was telling herself.

She said, "Well, I feel like an idiot. I have this horse whisperer chick standing behind me, and I don't think I am ever going to get this right."

I replied, "Is that what you meant by living large and loud? What will happen when you are standing in front of famous choreographers and directors, trying out new dances if this is what you are telling yourself?"

She replied, "It will suck."

I summed it up by saying, "Exactly." I also reiterated that this exercise with Yani was not about her being a horseperson. The exercise was about letting Yani be a mirror for Elisabeth to experience large and loud, so that the direction and energy would be alive and in her body when she arrived in New York.

She began the exercise again. As she began to get Yani moving, I said, "Elisabeth! Dance with that horse."

Elisabeth's energy changed completely from self criticism to pure joy. In seconds, Yani was galloping around the perimeter of the round pen at such a speed that she was hard to see, she was a blur. After a couple of laps, I asked Elisabeth to stand in the center of the round pen and take a deep breath. As soon as she did, Yani came to a dead stop, turned, and faced Elisabeth.

Elisabeth looked at me and burst out, "Now that was cool!"

My final remark was, "When you get to New York, remember this dance with Yani." When I last heard, Elisabeth was indeed living life large and loud, able to silence the voice of her inner critic whenever necessary. So why was Yani her teacher that day? Because Yani loves to dance! (Rocky, not so much).

Here are some questions for you to consider in creating a clear direction for yourself or your organization.

- What is the direction you want to take?
- What habits or beliefs do you need to let go of in order to move in that direction?
- Where might you be sending mixed messages about the direction you want to take?
- What would taking a step forward look like for you?

One of the activities we use as practice in our workshops for setting and maintaining a direction is a walking meditation in a labyrinth. A labyrinth is an intricate circular pattern drawn on the ground, representing the metaphor of a journey to the center of your life and then back out. People often confuse mazes and labyrinths. The major difference between the two is that there is no trick with a labyrinth, nothing to figure out. You simply follow the path through the winding, sometimes surprising, twists and turns, until you reach the center, then turn and walk the same path back out. The paths of most labyrinths are about two feet wide, enough for a person to walk comfortably. We built a labyrinth that is wide enough, five feet, for a person and a horse to walk together. We invite people to walk the labyrinth with the horse as their teacher, guide, and partner on their journey. We ask the participants to reflect on the direction they have set for their life, walk the path, and see what emerges for them to pay attention to in their time with the horse.

On a sunny summer Oregon afternoon, it was Nancy's turn to walk the labyrinth. The day was especially significant, because it was Lucky's first day as a full-fledged faculty member. Just before Nancy began her walk with Lucky, she shared with the group that she was struggling to keep herself and her husband focused on the new direction they had set for their business. Her husband would frequently get distracted with other opportunities, which was very frustrating for Nancy and hard on their relationship.

Then Nancy stepped onto the labyrinth leading Lucky, with him wearing a halter and lead rope. It wasn't long before Nancy was a few feet out in front of Lucky, and he was plodding behind her, quite disinterested. The parallel to her life was not lost on her, and none of us in the group had to say a word. Nancy slowed down, waited for this adorable little horse to catch up, and started again. She looked at Lucky with patience, love, and adoration.

Their walk proceeded along nicely for a few strides. Suddenly, Lucky stopped of his own accord, turned around completely, and began walking in the opposite direction. We all just stood there with our chins on the ground. Was this actually happening? Yes.

Nancy handled the situation in an amazing manner. In a calm, compassionate and reassuring voice, she said to Lucky, "Wait a minute honey, this way, we are going this way." She stopped and waited for Lucky to come back to her, with no indication of frustration. Lucky walked back to her and laid his head on her chest, at which Nancy gently cupped her hand around his cheek. After their shared moment of appreciation, they completed their walk without any more miscues.

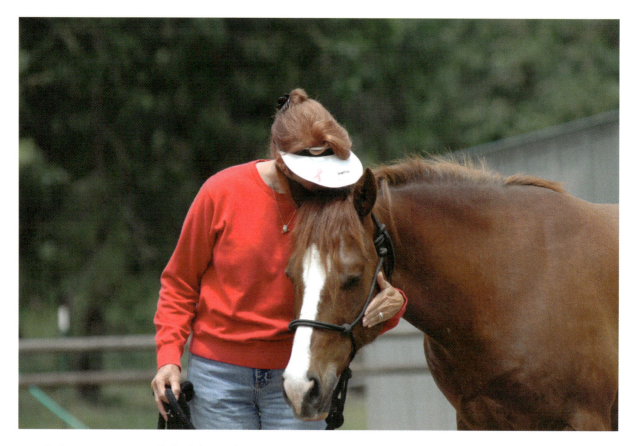

When Nancy exited the labyrinth and returned to where the group was standing, I said, "How might your husband feel if this is how you approached him when things get off track?"

Nancy said, "Oh my God, he would love it. That is probably just what he has needed all along."

As for Lucky, it was a glorious first day at school, and he loves being the teacher.

Energy
"Our anxiety tips us off to our aliveness." – Peter Koestenbaum

There is a growing awareness and understanding of how horses mirror and respond to energy. Because the true threats to our survival as human beings have been minimized, our consciousness of our energetic selves has diminished. We tend to focus more on our cognitive and intellectual capacities rather than on our energetic and feeling capacities. In many cases, we are unaware of the energy we bring into important situations in our lives.

I was asked to come and spend time with a minister, Laura, (also my sister) who was a former horsewoman and determined to reclaim her relationship with horses. She had recently purchased a horse named Sunny and was beginning to do groundwork with him to build their relationship. Doing groundwork was new to her and she wanted some coaching. At the time she and I met, she was stumped by an unexplainable reaction her horse was having when she would free longe (at liberty with no halter or lead line) him in the round pen. For some reason, every time she would ask him to move around her, he would only go at a full gallop and never at a walk or trot.

I asked her to take Sunny in the round pen and show me what she meant. As she walked to the center of the round pen, Sunny was on the outside rail, looking at her with anticipation. She was standing about ten feet from Sunny and positioned her body to face him, lining up her torso with his barrel. She began by raising her hand closest to his head to indicate the direction she wanted him to move -- like showing someone into an open door and saying, this way please. Then she raised her other hand, closest to his hip, to motion for him to move forward, giving him an energy cue from behind. When most people do this exercise in the round pen, they hold their hands near their waist. This minister held her hands in a "V" shape over her head and began walking at a moderate pace. In seconds, Sunny was galloping around her, just as she had described.

From outside the round pen, I simply said, "Try slowing down and lowering your hands."

She looked at me with a puzzled face and said, "What? I don't see what difference that would make…"

So I asked her to stop in the center of the round pen, drop her hands, and take a deep breath. As soon as she did, Sunny came to a complete stop.

I opened the gate to the round pen and went in. I said, "I am going to mirror for you what I just saw you do. Watch Sunny's reaction. Then, I am going to slow down and lower my hands. Watch Sunny's reaction."

When I held my hands above my head, Sunny galloped around me just as he had around Laura. I took a deep grounding breath and became centered. As I lowered my hands and slowed my pace, Sunny began to walk calmly around me. As Laura watched, I said, "What you were seeing is what Hallelujah looks like in the round pen."

She burst into laughter and said, "No wonder my staff keeps telling me I am hard to keep up with. That is the energy I bring to just about everything."

I left her with a question. Are there any situations in which the energy of the walk would be the right energy for you, your staff, and your community? Upon reflection, Laura shared with me that she realized her approach to leadership was taking people nowhere in a hurry. Since that day in the round pen with Sunny, Laura has radically altered the energy she brings to developing the leadership capability of her staff, so that their work together in the community will be sustainable, long after she is gone.

Here are some questions you can ask yourself to begin noticing the energy you bring to being a leader in your community:

- What gives you energy?
- What is draining your energy?
- What energy do you bring to leading your organization, community, or family?
- What is the focus of your energy at this point in your life?
- Is the focus of your energy aligned with the direction you want your life to take? If not, why not?

Rocky has taken my understanding of energy to an entirely new level. I have often hesitated to tell the stories of what I have seen him show people, because they sounded so unbelievable. Then I am reminded that I should tell these stories just for that reason, because we all need to move beyond disbelief in order to continue the journey of our evolution in consciousness.

Rocky has developed quite a reputation in my local community. His popularity has reached the point where people will call to see if they can come and spend time with Rocky. I leave that choice up to him. I received a call from a woman named Margaret who had attended an open house at our ranch several months earlier and witnessed Rocky's healing magic. First, I will tell you what she witnessed.

We hold open house events to educate the local community on the work we do with horses. As part of the event, we allow volunteers to engage in some of the Equine-Guided Education activities to get a feel for what the work entails. I am very careful not to call these events demonstrations. Anytime people work with horses, it is real for the horses, never just a show. When I ask for volunteers, I give people fair warning that they will be visible in front of the group and not to volunteer unless they are ready to be seen. Somehow I am never short of volunteers.

At this particular event, we had about thirty people show up, and the volunteer was an older gentleman named Ken. Ken stepped into the round pen with Rocky, and I began showing him how to get Rocky to accept his leadership by giving him clear direction with focused energy. When Ken felt safe to try it on his own, I stepped aside both to give him room to experiment and to share with the group my observations about what was happening in the exercise.

Ken's attempts to get Rocky moving felt forced and distracted. I coached him to move to the center of the round pen and start again when he felt clearer. As Ken stood calm and still in the center of the pen, Rocky walked over to him and began nuzzling Ken's right shoulder. The next thing I knew, tears were streaming down Ken's face. (This too is why we do not call them demonstrations.)

For this type of gathering, there was an uncharacteristically strong feeling of compassion and respect from the entire group for Ken. While he was in the round pen, you could have heard a pin drop. Focused on Ken, I said, "Tell us what is happening for you now."

Ken said with a quivering voice, "I can't."

I stepped closer to him and said, "Can you tell me?"

He nodded yes and began to tell me his story. When Ken was a young boy of about age eight, he had a horse-related accident. He and his brother were riding a horse together and they both fell off. Ken's brother was seriously injured and rushed to the hospital. What no one noticed was that Ken was also was injured. He had suffered a broken arm at his right shoulder. He walked around for days with this injury, and no one noticed because they were so focused on his brother. The spot that Rocky was nuzzling was the exact spot of the break.

Ken went on to say, "Something happened to me when Rocky touched my shoulder. After sixty years of carrying around this pain, it was gone. Gone." Rocky was the witness that Ken needed to let go of that old, emotional pain.

With Ken's permission, I turned to the group and told them his story. With not a dry eye among them, they burst into applause for Ken and for Rocky.

Now I will go back to Margaret. Margaret was profoundly affected by the healing she saw take place with Ken. So much so that nine or ten months later she called to see if she could bring a friend of hers who was being treated for cancer to come and visit Rocky. It was on a Saturday, and Margaret and her friend, Mary, were going to be in the area. I told them it was fine if they stopped by, but it would be Rocky's decision if he wanted to work on Saturday.

I walked out into the pasture where Rocky was grazing and began to talk to him about the people that were on their way. Standing beside him, I stroked his withers and said, "Rocky, two ladies want to come see you today. One of them is very sick. I know it is Saturday and if you don't want to work, it is okay with me. If you want to spend time with these ladies, come with me and I will get you cleaned up a bit before they get here." I began walking toward the gate. Rocky stopped grazing and came directly behind me.

When we got to the gate, I picked up his halter and lead line and walked him to our usual grooming area. I had no sooner brushed some dust off him when Margaret and Mary arrived. Rocky noticed the gate open to the driveway and followed the car with his eyes and entire body as they pulled toward and then past us into the parking area. The two ladies got out of the car and began walking toward us. Rocky let his gaze vacillate between the two women as if he was discerning which of them was here to see him. Suddenly, he locked onto Mary who was still thirty yards away from him.

I knew then that he was ready to go to work and that we needed to get past the introductions quickly. When they were in range of my voice, I began speaking. I said, "Hello ladies. As you can see, Rocky is already very interested in you and here is what you can expect. You have nothing to be concerned about.

You are completely safe with Rocky and me." I focused my attention on the woman Rocky was gazing at and said, "You must be Mary."

She said, "Yes, yes I am."

I then said, "Rocky is very focused on you, so I thought you might be the one that is here to see him. What Rocky will want to do as soon as you get close enough is to begin scanning your body with the tip of his nose. This is just his way of saying hello and getting to know you. When he is finished, we will all know it and we will go from there. How do you feel about that?"

Mary said, "Just fine. He is beautiful!"

Silence took over the conversation as Rocky began his process with Mary. With Mary facing him, he systematically scanned her entire body. He began by placing his nose about an inch away from her right foot, lifting his head ever so slowly up toward her right leg, moving all the way up over her right shoulder, across her neck, over and down her left side until he was back at the ground near her left foot. Then Rocky began raising his head back up her left side and stopped with his nose at her left breast. He then lifted his chin and laid it on her just above her breast. Mary then instinctively allowed her hand to rest on Rocky's forehead.

Seeing the partial weight of Rocky's head ever so gently next to her, I said, "This is where Rocky has chosen to stop. Tell me about that."

Mary replied, "I have breast cancer and have had a mastectomy of my left breast. Somehow with Rocky it doesn't bother me to say it."

As I saw a tear drop down her face, I said, "How do you feel right now?"

After a brief pause, she said, "Wonderfully light… and happy."

Rocky then took one step back, dropped his head, and began allowing his eyes to blink and close as if he was about to fall asleep. I asked Mary what she would like to do next, and she said with a glowing smile, "Just be here with him for a little while. Would that be okay?"

I said, "Absolutely."

With all of us in silence, Mary made her way around to stand beside Rocky and rested her hands on his back. After a few minutes with Rocky standing completely relaxed and still, Mary looked at me and said, "Thank you…so much."

Sensing that Mary felt complete, Rocky lifted his head, opened his eyes, and turned to me. Looking at Mary, I said, "You are so, so welcome."

The two ladies walked back to their car and drove away.

A few weeks later, Mary died. It was so heartening to know that she left this earth with at least one beautiful memory of being seen, not judged, having experienced the unconditional love and healing energy of our magnificent horse, Rocky.

As I reflected on this story, an important insight emerged. There is such simplicity and also mystery in this brief interaction. Two ladies came to my ranch on a Saturday, spent thirty minutes with Rocky and me, and then they left. I realized that the only way this profound connection and healing could have taken place in such a short amount of time was that everyone involved shared a belief that we are all connected. None of us had to explain or control what happened. Two ladies came to my ranch on a Saturday and spent thirty minutes with Rocky and me. In our time together, we shared the healing presence of a horse. The end.

Congruence
"We teach who we are." – Parker Palmer

My sister taught me that you do not find your purpose, you reclaim it. The thought behind that statement is that we are born congruent, with a unique purpose our lives are meant to fulfill. By congruent, I mean that our inner thoughts and feelings are aligned with our outer expression of those thoughts and feelings. Who we are on the inside and who we are on the outside are the same. As we go through life as children and then young adults living in an inauthentic world, we often lose sight of who we are and what we came into this world to be.

We begin learning how to become incongruent from very early in life. For instance, as a child, you might have entered a room where people like parents or teachers were in the midst of a conversation. You sensed that these people you cared about were in a fight. Although the conversation suddenly stopped when you walked in, somehow you still knew something was wrong. You were reading the energy in the room. You asked them, "What's wrong?"

And they replied, "Nothing."

That incident was your first lesson in learning to disregard your intuition or awareness of energy, and the precursor to living a life in incongruence. Such seemingly simple moments taught you important lessons that wound up as statements of warning from your inner voice to hide your real feelings, doubt your intuition, and above all else, keep silent about what you truly felt.

We live in a world that rewards incongruence. Think of the number of times you have said "yes" to people when you really wanted to say "no". We all know the standard, politically correct response to the greeting, "How are you?" "Fine, how are you?" Yet you know full well that "fine" is often not how you are feeling.

Our prevailing state of incongruence is the most important reason for turning to horses as our teachers. For horses, incongruence is not an option. As the author and horse trainer Chris Irwin put it, horses don't lie – ever. Horses tell you exactly what they are thinking and feeling, and express it through their body language. If a mare pins her ears to the back of her head and looks directly at another horse, she is clearly warning this horse that his behavior is unacceptable and will be punished with a swift kick if it continues. You can bet that other horse will not think this mare is kidding or lying. A horse that is stressed will have a high head and a tense neck. When horses lower their heads and relax their necks with a soft look in their eyes, they are feeling relaxed, comfortable, and safe.

When it comes to relating to human beings, horses would much rather be around someone who is congruent, no matter what the feelings may be. When someone is incongruent, for example, if they approach the horse with bravado while on the inside they are timid and unsure, the horse will act disinterested in them. If the horse could speak English, he would be saying something like "This person's inner energy and outer energies do not match. They do not know themselves; therefore, they are not to be trusted."

I have seen many people walk into the round pen with a horse at liberty, and the horse walks the opposite way. When this action happens, I ask people to become congruent. In other words, I ask them to talk about what really matters to them and what feelings are real for them right now. In becoming present with their true selves, people often lose track of where the horse is standing. Much to their surprise, when they become congruent, the horse suddenly looks up with interest as if to say, "Hello, when did you get here?"

In most cases, my horses then walk over and stand with the person. For many people, the experience is an affirmation of what can happen when they become congruent and of the freedom that comes with the honesty of being their true selves.

One of my clients, a physician named Rachel, came to a coaching session to work with the horses. As she described her frustrations, she said, "I just don't have time to connect with my patients."

I said to her, "Okay, we will make that the focus of our work today." I knew right then that Rocky was to be her teacher on this day. I led Rocky out of the pasture and into the breezeway of the barn. After the introductions were made and the safety guidelines understood, I instructed Rachel on how to groom Rocky.

Here is how the conversation went. "So Rachel, notice that Rocky is not dirty. This grooming exercise is not about you cleaning this horse. This exercise is about you relating to Rocky with the energy of connection."

Rachel nodded with understanding and immediately began scrubbing Rocky like he was being prepped for surgery.

Rocky began showing signs of discomfort and I quickly intervened. I said, "Rachel, it looks to me like you are working."

Rachel caught herself in a pattern. She looked at me with a telling frown accompanied with a slight exhale and said, "uh huh."

I asked her to take a big deep breath, center herself, and show Rocky the energy of connection. What happened next was extraordinary for everyone involved. In a moment of complete congruence, Rachel put down the brush, took a deep breath, closed her eyes, and then placed both of her hands on Rocky's barrel. It was as if the healing hands of God had landed on that horse. Every cell in his body relaxed. Rocky turned his head to her and engulfed Rachel in an authentic horse hug. As Rachel opened her eyes, tears were streaming down her face.

I simply said, "Tell me what is happening for you right now."

Rachel replied, "I could stand here all day."

I then proceeded to ask her an unexpected question. I said, "Have you ever met this horse before?"

Knowing I knew the answer to this question, she gave me a quizzical look with a furrowed brow and shook her head no.

My next question was, "How are you feeling toward Rocky?

She replied emphatically and with her arms now around his neck, "I love him!"

"Are you feeling connected to him?

"Yes!"

I replied with, "Hmmm, how long did that take?"

"Maybe five minutes."

As Rachel stood there looking at me, I said, "Connecting to your patients is not about time, it is about your intention. Reclaim your intention to connect with your patients from the second your eyes meet and you touch them with those healing hands."

So many of the caregivers I work with have chosen to become numb to deal with the realities of being in healthcare today. They dull themselves to the pain of the constant barrage of high patient volumes, ever-increasing demand, and never-ending media pot shots. The downside of being numb to pain is that joy goes with it. You cannot connect to people when you cannot feel.

Rachel's numbness fell away when she allowed herself to connect to Rocky. Rachel was able to reclaim her purpose as a caregiver and a healer. A few months later, she opened her own integrative medicine practice.

My friend and mentor Peter Block taught me a very important lesson. "Without no, yes is meaningless." Carolyn Resnick has taken my understanding of this notion even deeper. Resnick's Liberty Method of equine training is a process of developing a relationship with the horse (also referred to as the "Waterhole Rituals") without the use of tack, in other words, no halter, lead line, saddle, or bridle. The work to build the relationship is done with the person on the ground in a large area like a pasture or an arena, engaging in series of horse rituals that are used to establish the pecking order among members of a herd. Because the horses are at liberty, they are free to move and free to leave the relationship if they choose. Carolyn helped me understand what happens when you prevent a horse from moving. Horses speak to us with their bodies. When we constrain their movement, they can't talk. If we constrain their movement, they can't say no. So when they say yes, it's not really a true yes.

My understanding of the power of no came to life in my experience with my friend Lisa and her horse Ptarmigan. Lisa had an old story in her head about what it meant when Ptarmigan prances around, bucks, and kicks up his heels. She has been told on many occasions that her job was to bring him back in line whenever he displayed such boisterous behavior. In sharing the Resnick's Liberty Method of training with her, I engaged her in a conversation that reframed Ptarmigan's behavior.

I entered the round pen with Ptarmigan at liberty and began moving through the "Waterhole Rituals". I was establishing my position in the pecking order and asking him to accept my leadership. The first couple of times that I asserted my leadership by taking over the space he was standing in, he hopped away from me in a hilarious fashion and took off running with an emphatic "No".

Lisa was stunned by my reaction. All I did was laugh really loud and say to Ptarmigan, "You are really quite something." As he whipped around and faced me with a surprised look in his eye, I could tell he was not sure how to respond to my lack of anger and, indeed, my celebration of his dance.

As I took the next step in the ritual, I went up to greet him and say hello by stroking my hand down the center of his face. In the language of horses, this act is a statement that we are friends, not foes. The beauty of this ritual is that it reinforces that we are friends, but I am still the leader. To further demonstrate my leadership, I began herding him, demonstrating in the softest and most gentle way that I could move him in any direction with just my energy, communicating with my body in the language of horses. My question to him remained the same. "Will you accept my leadership?"

A few minutes later, he answered with a resounding "yes". His body language was completely transformed. His muscles relaxed. He dropped his head in contentment and became a willing partner.

As Lisa watched this transformation, she learned the power of celebrating this horse's choice to say "no" to being in service but to respond with a true "yes" to being in partnership. She let go of the judgment that he was being disrespectful and bad. Now it was her turn to dance the Waterhole Rituals with Ptarmigan. She stepped into the round pen and played for the very first time with the horse she had owned for years. In their exchange, Ptarmigan both respectfully and gracefully accepted Lisa's leadership, as did Lisa herself.

Here are some questions to help you on your path to becoming congruent again:
- What is your true nature?
- How do you typically mask your true self to the outside world?
- What are you trying not to feel?
- What is your authentic self trying to say?

One of the most profound moments of my life was a gift given to me from one of my former colleagues and still one of my best friends, Karen Kaufman. Karen and I had worked together for years when Yani came into my life. After work one afternoon, I invited Karen to come to the barn and meet Yani. When Karen arrived, I had already changed into my barn clothes, my usual jean shirt, wrangler jeans, cowgirl boots, and cowgirl hat. As Karen walked into the breezeway of the barn, I had Yani in hand. To this day, when I introduce a person to Yani, I will say, "This is Yani." I cannot say those three words without an undeniable grin on my face.

In response to those three words, Karen said, "I have known you, my dear June, for four years. Why is it that I feel like I am seeing you for the very first time?"

The only responses I could muster were an exhale, a smile, and a nod. There were no words required.

Community
"You do not have to ride a horse to have a relationship with it." – Neda DeMayo

It is my honor and privilege to introduce you to our last, but definitely not least, TeachingHorse faculty member. His name is Galen. Galen is a thirteen year old Oldenburg gelding standing eighteen hands high. This horse is seven feet tall and about eight feet long. I did not truly comprehend his scale when I agreed to meet him. Here is how it all started.

My sister Laura is the minister of All God's Children Church in Aulander, North Carolina. Aulander is one of the most impoverished communities in the state and this small country church is the lifeblood of the kids that live there. Laura knows that the children in the community she serves need a safe place to play and to develop their faith. She believes that, in order to meet the needs of the kids of today, this safe place will look different from a traditional church. She has envisioned creating "The Place of Possibilities" for over twenty years – a place where kids come to play basketball, learn to work with horses, eat warm meals, and be with people who will be there for them when they need it the most. Inspired by Laura's vision, a church in a nearby community had pulled a group of people together to help in raising money for The Place of Possibilities.

While preparing to meet with this group, Laura had a feeling in her heart that something important was going to be happening for some unknown person who would be at the meeting. When she started the meeting, she let the group know what she was feeling. She told the person to call her when they figured out who they were and she would be happy to support them on their journey.

A couple of weeks passed before a woman named Sandra called Laura and simply said, "I was the one you were speaking to in that meeting." After returning home from the meeting, Sandra received a call from the Oprah show wanting to know how much she would be willing to bid for an article of Oprah's clothing that would go to benefit a charity. Sandra is a huge Oprah fan and had been trying to get on the show for years. She was shocked when she heard herself saying, "$10,000.00."

The representative from Oprah said, "Great, you're in."

While Sandra was on the show, she won the bid on Oprah's little black dress. On her journey home, Sandra's thoughts began to come together and she had a clear sense of what she was to do. That's when she called Laura to tell her the story, and said she would like to hold a charity ball to raise money for The Place of Possibilities. The funds would be raised by an auction. The feature item for auction would be Oprah's little black dress.

When these events were transpiring, Laura and I were also collaborating on how to bring my work with horses to North Carolina and had developed a course to offer at The Place of Possibilities. The workshop, *SpiritHorse*, is designed for people on spiritual journeys from all walks of life who are looking to rejuvenate their passion to serve their communities. Wanting to support Laura's vision, I offered to contribute a

SpiritHorse course to the auction at the fundraising ball, named *The Little Black Dress Ball*. Laura and I met Lisa Wall, Galen's owner, for the first time at the ball. Lisa was the generous bidder on the *SpiritHorse* workshop. By the end of the evening, we were making plans to hold the workshop in the spring.

A few weeks prior to the workshop, Lisa and I spent some time together on the phone preparing for the event and discussing the horses that we would work with over the two days. During our talks, she told me about Galen. Galen's life had included some horrific experiences with aggressive and punitive trainers. Galen was trained as a dressage horse, as well as a hunter/jumper, neither of which he enjoyed. Lisa was committed to helping Galen find a purpose that he would love and that would honor his gifts. Galen is a people horse. Lisa understood the work of Equine-Guided Education and believed that Galen would be a perfect candidate. When she told me his story and asked me if I would be willing to work with him, I said, "Of course". When I arrived in North Carolina and met Galen for the first time, I will admit I was taken aback by his size. However, after a few short minutes of being in his presence, the only thing I could see was his heart.

In April, 2005, twelve people attended the first North Carolina *SpiritHorse* workshop held at Lisa's farm. It was a magical and moving experience for all involved. The work with the horses left everyone with deep insights about themselves. Lisa found that the experience allowed her to show her true horse self to her horses and her friends. She was no longer constrained by the image of being exclusively a dressage rider, but freed to fully be a horsewoman. Everyone was in awe of how the horses touched each person in a unique way, opening the path to authenticity in an amazingly short period of time. As you can probably guess, Galen was the star of the workshop. Lisa had been right, Galen was meant to be a TeachingHorse.

Lisa and I became good friends and kept in touch. And then one day, I got an unexpected phone call. Lisa had good news; she was happily expecting her third child. But at this point in her life, twelve horses were too many. Much to my surprise, the next thing out of her mouth was that she wanted Beth and me to have Galen. Lisa felt that Galen had never been happier than in the two days he had been a TeachingHorse faculty member. It was his destiny. I was speechless. Just a few months later, Galen began his journey from North Carolina to Oregon.

Lisa, being the dedicated horsewoman that she is, had many conversations with Galen about his new life on the horizon. She even enlisted the support of an animal communicator to try to understand how

Galen was feeling about the upcoming trip. Being around or in the pasture with other horses had generally made Galen very nervous and uncomfortable. Both Lisa and the animal communicator felt it would be best if Galen had his own pasture, where he could see other horses, but not be in the same pasture with them. Beth and I prepared a five acre pasture with a shelter fit for a king, just for him.

As serendipity would have it, Galen arrived only a few weeks after our new herd of wild horses had joined us. The pasture for Galen faced the pasture that Dream, Lucky, and Hope were in, but was separated by our driveway. Close, but not too close – just right, we thought. However Galen's first few weeks with us were quite stressful. We could not understand why he would pace the fence line of his pasture incessantly. As we understood it, Galen was accustomed to living in his own pasture, near, but not with, other horses. Even so, Beth and I began to believe that Galen had reached a point in his life where he wanted to be with other horses.

When Dream and her herd would graze over to the far side of the pasture where Galen could barely see them, he would let out the most longing and painful cries. They were not whinnies, they were cries. Hearing those cries, the mustangs would come running to comfort him. At night, Dream, Lucky, and Hope would stay close by, never getting far enough away to upset Galen. Then we noticed that Hope would stand directly across from Galen and match his every stride. She would steadily keep decreasing her pace until they both came to a stand still. Hope would just stand there with him, and Galen would finally stop pacing and rest.

As we were watching these dynamics emerge, I began to think it was time to try letting another horse in the pasture with Galen and see how things went. So, we brought in our bridge builder, Rocky. Since Rocky is very sure of himself and feels he has nothing to prove, we had a hunch that there would be little risk involved. What we saw when we led Rocky into the pasture was nothing short of amazing.

With his sore muscles and feet, Galen slowly made his way over to the gate. Rocky walked in calmly with a level head, and then lowered his head, almost to the ground, as he approached Galen. Galen matched his move, and they met nose-to-nose for the first time, about two inches from the ground. Size did not matter. Rocky turned and headed for the most luscious part of this pasture, a space that Galen had never adventured over to see. Galen followed in behind him, and they began a lovely afternoon graze. There were no fireworks, not even a squeal. Beth and I just stood there, stunned. We were so moved, and also relieved.

Just when we thought everything was going to be okay, Galen headed back over to the fence line and began calling for the mustangs. Of course, Hope was the first one to arrive. It was then that it hit me. Galen doesn't just want to be with other horses, he wants a girl! Even so, I was not ready to make that big of a move just yet. We let Rocky and Galen stay together for a few weeks to see if things would stay as peaceful as they had began. As you can imagine, we were also constantly on the phone with Lisa with a detailed play-by-play. She was thrilled that Galen finally had a friend he felt safe with and Rocky was her hero, as well as ours.

Rocky began to give Galen some early lessons in how to be a horse. It's quite common for horses in a herd to reprimand each other for behaviors that could compromise the safety of the herd, and Rocky had had just about enough of Galen's pacing. To end the pacing once and for all, Rocky would run to the end of Galen's pacing pattern and stop, turn his butt to Galen, and essentially dare him to take another step. Then Galen would turn and go the other way. Rocky would run past him to the other end, turn his butt to Galen, and plant his defiant hooves! As soon as Galen would turn, off Rocky would go again, shortening the end of the line each time. Finally, Galen had no room to turn, so he decided to just put his head down and graze on the spring grass. I could feel Rocky's inner voice saying, "It's about time, you big dumbass."

A few weeks had passed with Galen and Rocky sharing a pasture without incident, so we decided that it was time to introduce Galen to the mustangs and see how it went. Beth and I took a few big deep breaths, and we both led Galen into the mustangs' pasture. As Galen entered the gate, Hope lifted her head from the grass and let out a soft, low, melodic nicker. Galen immediately dropped his head and returned the greeting. At this point, the horses in this little herd, not one of them over 14.5 hands, made their way closer to Galen. The energy was magnetic but not the least bit tense. I untied Galen's halter and let it drop off him and into my hands. Beth and I moved back toward the fence.

Hope was the first to approach Galen. It was as if they had both been waiting for this moment. Hope lifted her head and extended her neck out to greet him. Galen lowered his head and extended his nose to hers with a noticeable feeling of love and respect. In the next instant, Hope turned to face Dream and Lucky, with her ears pinned signaling to them to approach with caution. They both slowly, and with one eye on Hope, said a quiet hello to the gentle giant. Galen stood completely still. After the greetings,

Hope turned to resume grazing with Galen following close behind. Now Galen was happy. As Beth and I watched this gracious acceptance of Galen into this herd, our eyes welled up with appreciation. When we were certain everything was going to be okay, we ran in the house to call Lisa and tell her that Galen officially had a girlfriend and a herd.

If you can believe it, it gets even better. The pasture the mustangs lived in was adjacent to the pasture where Yani's herd grazes during the day. The next day when we brought Yani and her herd in to graze, Harley made a beeline for Galen. With only a fence line between them, it would have been easy for them to get into a fight since Harley was intent on keeping any strange male horse away from his precious Yani and baby Grace. But this fight was never going to happen, Hope and Dream made sure of that. What happened next was something I would not have believed if I had not seen it with my own eyes. Hope and Dream herded Galen into their loafing shed where Harley could not reach him. Harley just stood at the fence line, staring Galen down. Meanwhile Yani proceeded to take her cue from Dream and Hope. Yani maneuvered herself between Harley and the fence line, and with pinned ears and a swift threatening kick, she demanded that Harley be on his way. The mares had spoken. Gentlemen, there will be no fighting.

This same ritual took place for weeks. Harley would gallop to the fence line and Hope and Dream would herd Galen away. Finally Galen would just go into the loafing shed on his own whenever Harley was coming. After a couple of days of this uneventful submission, Harley relaxed and began to trust that Galen was no threat to his herd. These days you will see frequent greetings, nose-to-nose, over the fence with no issues.

In her book *Naked Liberty*, Carolyn Resnick emphasizes again and again that the job of herd leadership is to create harmony and unity. As I watched these horses become a herd, a community, I truly understood what Carolyn meant. Mare wisdom and leadership are what created this healthy, sustainable community.

I have learned yet another very important lesson about community from these extraordinary horses. The lesson is about rituals and having fun. As part of our summer routine of rotating pastures, Dream and her herd created quite a ritual for themselves. Every afternoon we would take Yani and her herd from the front pasture and put them in their stalls for the evening. Once they were all settled, we would open the gate to the fence from the back pasture to the front pasture. Dream, Hope, Lucky, and Galen would race to see who could make it to the front of the pasture first. It was a glorious race filled with midair leaps, exuberant kicks, and thundering hooves. Beth and I stopped whatever we were doing to watch and cheer for the day's frontrunner. Of course Dream won the first few races, but that did not last for long. Hope soon took her share of the first place finishes. When Hope got to within a nose of Dream, she kicked into a whole new gear with such intensity and focus that it was a sight to behold. Lucky had a cunning way of positioning himself to get a head start. When he won, all thirteen hands of him crossed the imaginary finish line with flaring nostrils and a prideful post-win prance. Galen, bless his heart, was usually six of his lengths behind due to his long body and air-filled, former dressage horse strides. Then one day, it finally happened. Beth and I were in the pasture, cleaning out the mustangs' and Galen's shelter when we looked up in both disbelief and shock. Galen was winning the race. He had changed his stride completely to match the quick, close-to-the-ground strides of the mustangs. Galen was running like the wind. Beth and I threw down our pitch forks and began clapping and yelling, "Go, Galen, go!" He reached the finish line a nose in front of Hope. Not only had these mustangs taught Galen how to live in a herd, they had also taught him how to run!

For the next several weeks, just as fall was turning into winter, the entire herd of four would arrive at the finish line neck and neck. The ground was beginning to harden as the night and morning frosts were beginning to cover the grass. We had a long cold snap with temperatures dropping into the low twenties for several weeks in a row. The ground was bricklike. At this point, Galen bruised his hoof and developed an abscess. I noticed that he had a bit of a limp and called the vet. The usual process took place. The abscess was drained, cotton and betadine were packed into the wound, and a course of antibiotics was administered together with an anti-inflammatory to take the pain away. Galen would be good as new in no time, but for the next few days, he would not be up for the race.

The following day, I went to open the gate between the pastures, which was the proverbial starting gate. But there would be no race today. Dream, Hope, and Lucky walked slowly and steadily to the front of the pasture, making sure that Galen never felt alone or left behind. I was forever touched by this display of community. Looking into that herd with its one giant and three tiny horses is like looking at family members who you would swear could never be related. Yet, they are undeniably a family. Those two blood sisters and a brother have embraced Galen as one of their own in their every action and deed. That is community. That is why they are all considered the distinguished faculty of TeachingHorse.

P.S. The *Little Black Dress Ball* was a huge success. What began as an idea Sandra and her friends discussed over coffee at her kitchen table grew into the charity and social event of the year. Over six hundred people including state and local dignitaries were in attendance. Oprah's dress, purchased at the show for $3,800.00, was sold at auction for $13,000.00 and went on to be the centerpiece of another charity event to benefit the restoration of a house that was a stop on the Underground Railroad. Enough money was raised to fund The Place of Possibilities.

Grace

"I am not a horse trainer. I am a horseman. A horse trainer trains horses. A horseman trains himself."
– Chris Cox

I can honestly say that I have lived a life full of grace. From the time I was a little girl, I have felt blessed by the feeling of a Spirit watching over me. My Mother gave me a sense of faith and I am only today beginning to understand its depths. My father instilled in me the belief that, "To whom much is given, much is expected," along with a deep commitment to let my divine calling be what guides my every step. Even so, I have never lived under the illusion that a life full of grace is not without adversity, struggle, and change. The writing you are reading now is different from what you have read in the previous chapters. In the earlier pages, I was writing about what had happened in my life and in my relationship with horses. Now I am writing about what is happening real-time. It is much more difficult.

Almost two years ago, I began a journey with a prayer and the clearest vision I have had in twenty years. I asked God for Grace. While Yani was at Ariana's ranch, she lived in a pasture beside a mare and foal, Ruby and Sunny. Living next to this little foal as he grew was Yani's greatest pleasure. She followed his every move, and Ruby was gracious enough to allow it. Yani is never subtle in telling you what she wants. On numerous occasions while I was visiting her at the barn, she would look at the baby, look at me, then look back at the baby, then back to me, over and over again. Finally I said to her, "Yani, do you want one of those?"

She batted her irresistible soft brown eyes at me, dropped her head, and relaxed as if she was confident I had finally gotten the message.

After we had been settled at Grace Mountain Ranch for a year or so, Beth and I set out on the task to find Yani just the right stud and the final decision was, of course, hers. We were blessed to find the perfect stud only a few miles from our home. When the time came to make the final choice, the breeder led Yani into the breezeway of her barn where there were two stallions, one at each end. She led Yani to the first stall to meet option number one, a three year old, huge paint stallion named Charger.

Upon this introduction Yani proceeded to turn her self around and then double barrel kicked Charger's stall door.

I looked at the breeder as she regained her composure and said, "That was a 'no'."

So we moved along to the other end of the barn to meet the other option, a seasoned, gentle, gorgeous tobiano paint stallion, affectionately referred to as Bear.

Yani approached him with a glimmer in her eye and uttered a soft sultry nicker that was most definitely an invitation. I said to the breeder, "That was a 'yes'."

I got a call from the breeder the next day saying that Yani had been "as hot as a pistol," and they were pretty sure she would be pregnant. That was on May 15, 2005.

That night, in my most prayerful way, I began envisioning a little paint horse filly, her coloring vivid white mixed with Yani's copper-like buckskin distinction, dancing around the pasture. I imagined her in great detail, seeing her face for the very first time and saying, "Hello Grace." Knowing that the typical gestation period is eleven months, I immediately began informing people that I would not be available for work or travel starting in April, 2006. I wanted to be there for the birth. I took about six weeks off from work, confident that would be enough time. I waited and waited. The time came when I was running out of cash and client patience, and needed to get back to work. I finally had to leave to work with a client on May 2–5. Consumed with a sense of scarcity, I agreed to travel to a client engagement located about six hours from our ranch. As I drove away, I left daunted with the fact that I was leaving Yani at this most vulnerable time. I came home with $4,500.00, and I can promise you it was not worth it. Grace was born on May 4, 2006. I missed her birth by one day. I was completed devastated, sitting alone in a hotel room, when I got the call from Beth that Yani had delivered around 11:00 P.M. I drove home the next night.

The good news was that the birth had been an easy one for Yani and Grace. Beth had called my hotel at 10:30 P.M. to let me know that all was well and that there was no baby yet. Thirty minutes went by. Beth had gone outside for one last check and was greeted with two pairs of eyes rather than one. After an initial panic, a few rounds of "Oh my God," and a phone call to our vets, Beth called me back at 11:00 P.M. While she was standing outside with our vets, Yani, and the new baby, I had to know three things. Were they both okay, was it a girl, and what color was she? Aside from me not being there, my prayer, my vision, and my dream had come true.

I arrived at the barn the next night. I remember walking to the barn and Yani beginning to nicker at me as I approached. As I leaned over the stall door to put my hands on Yani and to tell her how much I loved her and how proud I was of her, I saw two very familiar soft brown eyes open to look at me for the first time. It was finally my time to say, "Hello Grace." I could not have been more touched or honored when she stepped away from her mother's strong, protective chest, with a bit of an exuberant hop, to stretch out her soft tiny nose to me. Not wanting to intrude too much on their initial bonding time, I kissed them goodnight and told Yani, "Grace is beautiful, and as always, so are you. Congratulations. I will see you two in the morning."

I waited until the next day to make my apologies to Yani and to Grace for not being there. We had configured a large outdoor area that Yani's stall opened onto for the two of them to be able to move around together and get some sunshine. Sitting on a straw bale, I leaned over with my elbows on my knees, my head down, and I said the words, "I am so sorry." When I opened my eyes, Grace had laid her head on my shoulder. I am so glad that Beth was standing there with the camera.

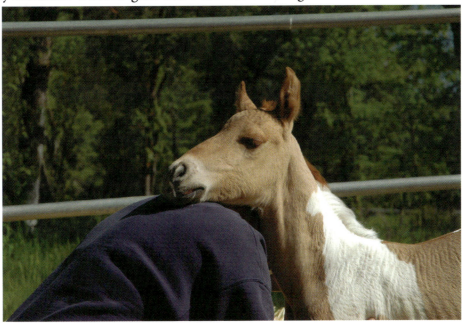

Being with Yani and Grace for the last year has been one of the greatest gifts of my life. Participating in raising this baby horse has required me to elevate my skill as a horse person to an entirely new level. I have grown even more as a person and as a leader. Everyday with Grace is a lesson in closing the gap between who I am now and who I am becoming.

I have had to endure agonizing emotional pain in service of doing what was right for my herd. For starters, I had to separate Harley from Yani. As Yani was preparing to foal, I let Harley be in a pasture adjacent to Yani's foaling area. Separated by only a pasture fence, Harley would not leave Yani's side. He had grazed down the pasture in the area close to her, and still he would not leave. He would stand watch, never lying down as he usually does at night. He was exhausted. On the night Grace was born, Beth had to move Yani and the baby up to another barn to help keep them both warmer and drier. Harley was a wreck. But somehow over the next few days, Harley relaxed. He seemed to know that Yani needed space to be with Grace and not have the stress of having to protect her, even from him.

After a couple of months, we were able to reintegrate Yani and Grace with Harley and Rocky. Harley was so happy to have Yani back. I did not even realize just how dull he had become until I saw his majestic light reappear the instant Yani walked through the gate into his pasture. It was then he earned his name change from Harley to "Big Daddy". We have all been so touched by his patience and gentleness with Grace.

Our next challenge was the weaning process. When Grace was about five months old, Yani began losing weight very rapidly. As I looked at Yani, I knew it was time to wean Grace. We orchestrated the weaning in the most gradual and systematic way to make it as least traumatic as possible. Even so, listening to that baby cry for her mother, knowing that I was the one leading her away from her, just about broke me. Again, thank God for Rocky.

Rocky was Grace's official babysitter and he did a phenomenal job. When they say it takes a community to raise a child, they are right, and it takes a herd to raise a baby horse. What made this part of the process successful was the strength of the bond in place between Rocky and Yani. By this time, Yani was ready for a break from Grace. Because of the months that Grace had spent bonding with Harley and Rocky, the adjustment of just being with Rocky for a while was not too difficult. Yani never showed any concern about Grace being with Rocky.

Rocky then took it upon himself to gradually educate Grace on embracing her independence. As part of our new morning routine, I would first lead Rocky from the barn to their pasture. Then I would lead Grace. For the first few weeks, Rocky would stand at the gate and wait for Grace to arrive. One day, he decided he would be about twenty yards away from the gate, still in full view, already grazing when Grace arrived. A few weeks later, Rocky would be behind a group of trees and a bit harder to see. Grace would have to get past her anxiety, calm herself down, begin sensing where he was, and then find her own way to him. As a result, Grace grew more self confident every week. It was an extraordinary process to watch.

The time finally came when the weaning was done and we could reintegrate the herd once again. As we led Rocky and Grace back into the main pasture with Yani and Harley, something happened that we did not expect. Yani came running over to reassert herself as Grace's mother, delivering several threatening kicks in Rocky's direction. The only way I can describe Rocky's reaction is in human terms. In classic Rocky fashion, he turned his butt to Yani, planted his immovable hooves into the ground, and essentially said in horse, "You have got to be kidding me. I have just spent the past four months taking care of your often irritating child, who is now my baby too by the way! I just don't think so, Missy. Back off!"

Harley, frankly, just decided to stay out of this one. We all had to remember that Yani was a first-time mother and she was still figuring things out herself. Within a few minutes, they all started to settle down. Yani received a very clear signal when Grace decided to go off to graze with Rocky. This little act of Grace ended that conversation once and for all. Now they are back in the groove as a family of four.

I have learned lately that leading a ten month old filly from place to place is akin to parenting a teenager, complete with an abundant dose of boundary testing. I have learned more about paying attention, giving clear direction with focused energy, and being congruent than I ever anticipated in this process. What you need to know about this time in my life is that there is no shortage of potential distractions. We are preparing to move from Oregon to North Carolina. Our time at Grace Mountain Ranch has been glorious, but now it is time for us to be closer to our family in North Carolina. We have been in the midst of all of the chaos of preparing the Oregon ranch to be sold, realtors and buyers constantly casing the property, trips to North Carolina to find a new home for us all, as well as keeping our business running at the same time. We have been struggling to find the right house with enough land and equestrian facilities.

This particular morning was a hard one for me. As you have read, we have many lovely rituals at our Oregon home. When I lead Rocky and Harley from the barn to their pasture in the morning, they race from one end to the other in a very brotherly competition. As I watched them this morning I found myself thinking in a bit of frustration, "Enjoy that while you can fellows, you might be running in a circle if our pastures in North Carolina aren't quite this big."

Then I led Yani down. In an uncharacteristic fashion, when Yani got into the pasture, she began running around in circles at a blazing speed, interspersed with a few leaps, bucks, and farts. Like I said, Yani is not subtle in telling you what she thinks or wants.

By this point, Grace, who was waiting to be led from the barn to the pasture, had seen and felt all of those energetic exchanges and was beyond the point of being able to contain her adolescent self. Our walk from the barn to the pasture looked like an awkward horse and human version of the tango mixed in with a little square dancing in a circle. I became completely present in the moment, with no other thought in my head than guiding Grace and bringing her back to a calm, respectful state. I had to stay relaxed to be able to move my body fluidly in response to hers, to keep both her and me safe. I had to keep directing Grace and moving her with my energy, without making her anxiety worsen. I had to be completely congruent, not trying to mask my own anxiety with superficial and unauthentic statements to her like, "It's okay, you're okay." That would have been futile. Instead using my words, energy, and guidance as calmly and gently as I could, I said to her, "Grace, the way you are reacting now is not okay. Until you calmly and respectfully walk with me, like we have been practicing for months, I will not let you in the pasture."

To further my development during this leadership lesson, Yani, Rocky, and Harley began racing around in response to all of Grace's antics. My message to them was the same, "Until you all calm down, I am not letting Grace in."

After a few snorts and exhales from the three of them, they simply became more interested in grazing than watching Grace and I tango. Shortly thereafter, Grace settled down and gained her composure. Once we had walked together for several minutes in a well-mannered way, I quietly led her into the pasture. Grace walked in and nonchalantly started grazing with her herd as if nothing had happened a few seconds ago. I said, "Good girl", then walked in the house and sat down to drink my now cold cup of coffee, completely exhausted.

As I sat there, it hit me. What I went through this morning demonstrates why many people don't necessarily find learning how to pay attention that attractive. Paying attention, being completely present with a heightened sense of awareness, able to move in any direction at a moment's notice, then immediately relax and let whatever just happened go is incredibly hard work. This experience gave me even deeper respect for the wisdom of horses. Horses live this way twenty-four hours a day. I lived it for forty-five minutes and was absolutely spent. That same afternoon, my walks with everyone, even with Grace, from the pasture to the barn were pleasant and uneventful. I have no idea what tomorrow will hold, but you can bet I will not let myself be preoccupied with real estate-related frustrations. I must simply be relaxed and ready – again.

The Way Closing

"Happiness requires a certain surrender. You have to give up your idea of happiness in order to discover what happiness is." – John Tarrant

About a year ago, I was spending some quality time in a small foaling pasture with Yani when she was about to give birth. It was a beautiful spring day and we were both enjoying the warm sunshine we had not seen in several months during the Oregon rainy season. Suddenly, a tremendous storm came in out of nowhere. We moved into her foaling shed that had a tin roof. I had never actually stood under a tin roof in the middle of a hail storm before. It was deafeningly loud!

I looked at the sky behind us and could tell that the storm would not last long. In an attempt to comfort Yani through the wind, rain, and hail, I said, "This one won't last long, girl. I am right here. The sun will be over our shoulders in no time. We should keep an eye out for a rainbow. Look for the rainbow, Yani." She peered out from behind me as if she knew what I was saying.

The storm ended quickly and we emerged out from under the shelter. Again I said, "Look for the rainbow."

We had gotten soaked before we could get to the shed and now there was a cloud of steam rising off Yani's back. As I stood beside Yani with my hand pressed against her shoulder, a rainbow did in fact emerge, but it was not in the sky. The rainbow was over Yani. It began about three inches from her nose, arched about two feet over her body, and ended over the base of her tail. As the rainbow hung in mid air over her body, all I could say was, "Look, there it is. Can you see it?"

My greatest hope was that Yani felt it. I know I did. In a perfect peaceful moment, we were surrounded by a complete spectrum of light, borne out of a moment of pelting uncertainty. In the midst of the sleepless nights and human worries that come with preparing for the birth of a foal, I am pretty sure I was the one who needed the reminder to look for the rainbow.

It is so easy to forget that most extraordinary acts of creation were preceded by acts of destruction, order emerging from chaos, rainbows appearing after a storm. If you had told me a year ago that I would be preparing to leave this sacred land we call Grace Mountain Ranch, I would have told you were crazy. Yet here I sit, on the verge of chaos once again. If nothing else, it has been a reminder that nothing in life is permanent. I am also quite clear that my leadership, the trust my herd places in me, and my faith are about to be tested once again. Any day now, I will be loading my herd onto a tractor trailer and driving with them across the country from Oregon to our new home in North Carolina. It feels like I am leaving the cocoon that was created to turn this motley crew of two people, eight horses, eight cats, and four dogs into a family, and the land that was the birthplace of TeachingHorse.

I also feel that I am being called home. I spent the first thirty-two years of my life growing up in North Carolina. So much of the person I am and my identity is tied to those Southern roots. My herds, both human and animal, past and present, currently living in now disparate corners of the country, are about to converge. Many of my dearest friends and family members have never met Yani or any of the horses in our herd. I can't wait to say the words to each of them, "This is Yani." Followed very shortly by, "And here are Rocky, Harley, Grace, Dream, Lucky, Hope, and Galen."

I also will not deny the magnitude of trepidation and vulnerability coursing through my veins. It has been one thing for this herd of horses to trust my leadership within the safety of our sacred cocoon. I am very aware of the reality that it will be quite another thing for me to keep the trust and confidence of this herd as we are catapulted into unfamiliar territory.

Truthfully, there is an element of leaving this place that feels like a failure. Being able to make a living in Oregon has not been easy. I have taken great solace from a quotation from Carolyn Resnick's book *Naked Liberty* where she writes, "The importance of failure is that it will guide you to seek the kind of help that will really empower you."

Many years ago my friend Peter Block said to me, "Faith is when you pursue your purpose without proof that it will provide for you." Now I can honestly say that I know what he means and I wouldn't change a thing. I have never felt more alive or more agile in my entire life. Relaxed and ready? Always a work in progress.

The synchronicity of some recent events has been both challenging and intriguing. We labored over the decision to leave Grace Mountain Ranch, but once we made the decision, we were hoping that the process would move quickly. Our hopes were to no avail. We went through a long period with our house on the market, offers that fell through, and back up offers that came just in the nick of time. On the downside, I am the kind of person who likes to rip off a Band-aid rather than strip it off slowly and gently. On the upside, I am able to entertain the notion that these last few months here have been given to us for a reason. I discover the reasons daily.

I owe a debt of gratitude to a very special person and gifted horse trainer, Jami Butler. Jami has been both my guide and partner in starting Dream, Lucky, and Hope under saddle. While I was completely confident in teaching these young horses their ground manners, leading in hand, and liberty work, I had never started a horse under saddle and wanted the help of an expert. I have learned so much from being a part of the process and was shameless in accepting Jami's offer to take the first few rides. Because we have taken our time and moved at a pace that fit the needs of each horse, the experience for them has been without trauma, even interesting and enjoyable.

One afternoon when we were working with Hope, I asked Jami what I knew was a dangerous question. I asked her, "So, how long do you think it will be before Hope is ready for me to ride her?"

The suspicion in my gut was confirmed when Jami said, "Oh, you can ride her now. Do you want to get on?"

Needless to say, there was a long pause. Hope turned her head to look at me with her precocious brown eyes. I never did say anything in response to Jami's question. I just got up off my seat and headed for them as Jami dismounted. I knew in my heart that this was the day and this was the time for me to ride Hope. Surprisingly, I felt perfectly calm from the moment I placed my foot in the stirrups and sat down on her back. We had a lovely, uneventful, first ride together.

As Hope and I meandered quietly around the riding arena, Lucky strolled up to the gate, watched us, and waited for us to finish. I opened the gate to let Hope back into the pasture, and Lucky walked in.

It is important to note that Lucky was considerably less ready than Hope and Dream to accept the saddle. Yet over the past few weeks, something had shifted in him and he seemed to be getting past some of his previous anxieties. To orient Lucky to having a rider, Jami removed the saddle and mounted him bareback. The process was very gradual, beginning with leaning on him, scratching his back, putting a little of her body weight on him, then laying her body over him. Finally she had one leg over each side while laying her body close to his neck and eased her way into sitting upright on him. During this time, I stood with Lucky holding his halter and lead rope, rubbing his head and talking to him. With the combination of all of the scratching and the warm spring sun, Lucky almost fell asleep during the process.

On the same day that I rode Hope, Lucky not only accepted the saddle with relative ease, he also accepted Jami as a rider. It is such a gift to know that Dream, Hope, and Lucky will be ready for the next step in their adventures by the time we leave the cocoon as well.

There is so much work that goes into preparing horses to move confidently through a strange human world. I am particularly concerned about how the trip will be for Grace. Everything she encounters on the journey will be a first for her. To make the experience as easy as possible, we have begun the process of desensitizing her to some of the typical objects she may see such as plastic bags, tarps, barrels, and cones. The goal of the desensitization process is to teach Grace to respond to unfamiliar objects in ways that keep both her and us safe. What we have discovered is just how brave she already is and the unusual level of confidence and self control she possesses as a yearling.

Throughout this process, I have drawn from the wisdom of many of my teachers and mentors. In his book *Let Your Life Speak*, Parker Palmer tells the story of how one of his Quaker community mentors, Ruth, helped him deal with closing doors. Ruth's words were, "There is as much guidance in the way that closes behind us as there is in the way that opens ahead of us. The opening may reveal our potentials while the closing may reveal our limits." We leave this mystical cocoon ready to discover our potential.

To honor both the closing of this phase of our lives and the exciting new opening, we named our new ranch in North Carolina "Southern Grace," home of TeachingHorse. Now more than ever, the world needs to learn what horses know.

When I was in my twenties, I said to my mother, "Mom, I don't think I am going to have children."

She replied, "You will have thousands."

We need to be teaching our children how to live in the moment and pay attention to what is happening around them. We must teach the coming generations how to set a clear direction for their lives and to make conscious choices about the energy they bring into their relationships and communities. Our job is to create communities that encourage congruence over incongruence and that honor the true nature of each unique individual. For our children and our communities to learn these vital lessons, we must all become the leaders they deserve.

Conclusion: Horse Sense

"It may be that when we no longer know what to do, we have come to our real work, and that when we no longer know which way to go, we have begun our real journey."
— Wendell Berry

The MareWisdom model answers the question, what do horses know about leadership? For a horse to be chosen as a lead mare, she must demonstrate four capabilities.

1. The lead mare must be paying attention and able to detect even the most subtle changes in the environment.
2. The lead mare must give the herd clear direction on where to go next.
3. The lead mare must be able to follow that direction with focused energy, providing the herd with guidance on the pace (i.e., walk, trot, canter) with which to respond to those changes.
4. The lead mare must also show the congruence of her inner and outer expressions. Her body language expresses what she is thinking, and she never lies. She has the herd's best interest as her sole source of motivation at all times.

Attention, direction, energy, congruence: when a lead mare demonstrates these capabilities, the herd becomes confident in her leadership. Confidence in the lead mare makes the herd agile in times of change, no matter how uncomfortable it may be.

June Gunter, Ed.D.

My best teachers have been the ones who were willing to make me uncomfortable. In one of my riding lessons with Ariana, she was teaching me to trust my body and my connection to the horse, more than my saddle horn and stirrups, when the unexpected arrived. While I was riding Yani around the arena at a walk, Ariana suggested that, when I was comfortable, I take my feet out of the stirrups and just let my legs dangle. Taking my feet out of the stirrups would allow my body to move more fluidly with Yani's body, making it more likely for me to be able to stay with her if she moved suddenly, instead of tensing up and moving against her.

With a moderate degree of reservation, after all we were just walking around in the arena, I tried it. I was amazed at the difference in our shared rhythm and the connection of my body to hers.

Ariana's next suggestion was that I put my feet back in the stirrups and increase our pace to a trot. Again she said, "Now, when you feel comfortable, keep moving at a trot and take your feet out of the stirrups."

My inner voice began to sound like a fire alarm essentially saying, "You are crazy!" To get past my fear, I had to have a very serious conversation with myself. I said to myself, "Come on. What is the worst thing that can happen in this sand filled arena? You are not out on the trail alone. You have learned a lot and Yani is completely calm. You can do this." After a couple of laps at the trot, I took my feet out of the stirrups. What I remember most is how much fun I was having – how much fun we were having.

After both Yani and I crossed this very important threshold, Ariana presented us with yet another opportunity. She said, "Go ahead and pick up the canter."

With my feet in the stirrups, Yani and I began to canter around the arena. Now, even with my feet in the stirrups, our rhythm was much more in sync than we had ever experienced before. Just as I was starting to feel comfortable, Ariana said, "Okay, when you are ready, take your feet out of the stirrups."

I think the words "No way" must have shot through every cell in my body, because without being cued, Yani came to a screeching halt. Ariana laughed out loud and then, so did I.

It was time for another conversation with my inner voice. My inner voice, the one that lives in my body and remembers what it feels like to fall, was screaming, "You are going to die!" In order to quiet the voice of my fears, I needed to hear the voice of my passion and purpose. I was determined to be the rider that Yani deserved. If we were going to have a real partnership, I had to get past this old fear in my body.

For Yani to ever really accept me as her leader, I had to get past my fear of falling and focus on riding no matter where the road took us.

I took a deep breath to remember why this ride was so important. We started again and I cued Yani to pick up the canter. The time came when we felt in rhythm, in unison, and I let my feet fall out of the stirrups. I was no longer riding Yani; we were dancing. Suddenly everything we had been through was worth it, no matter how uncomfortable we had to be, to get to this one moment of perfect partnership. For this dance to happen, I had to clear my mind of anything but the present moment and pay attention, set a clear direction for us, and let the energy of the canter flow through my body. My motivation had to be pure, to move us forward in our relationship, to gain Yani's confidence in me as a leader, rather than simply improve my ability as a rider.

Our society will regain trust and confidence in leadership when leaders are defined as those who you know are paying attention to what is going on in their business or community, are able to give clear direction with focused, inspiring energy, and are so authentic that you never worry about whether you can trust their intentions.

However, even with a new model of leadership, the question remains. What will make the life of a leader sustainable? How do we get beyond the clichés that it is lonely at the top and there is no rest for the weary?

I learned another profound leadership lesson from watching Yani with her herd. When the lead mare of a herd is tired, she rests, and there is no shame in asking someone else to step up and lead. When Yani was in her eleventh month of pregnancy, she was no longer fit to be the leader of the herd. Yani had "pregnant brain" and was tired and uncomfortable. Because she lived in a herd with two geldings, there was not another mare to ask to step into her shoes. So Yani offered her leadership position to Rocky. In a herd gallop very intentionally initiated by Yani, she waited for Rocky to take the lead and then slowed to a complete stop. Ordinarily, if Rocky had tried to pass her, Yani would have pinned her ears and kicked at him – not today. Rocky was immediately clear on what was being asked of him. In celebration, Rocky pranced around Yani as she stood perfectly still. Then Rocky set a direction for the herd and led them off to graze in the pasture. Yani spent the next several months devoted to her new life as mother.

Rocky held the leadership of the herd until Yani's new foal, Grace, was about seven months old. When Grace was strong enough to keep pace with the herd on her own, Yani initiated another herd gallop and blew past Rocky with her typical blazing speed. When they reached the end of the pasture, Yani and Rocky met nose-to-nose with bowed heads. It was clear to me that Yani was saying, "Thank you."

Rocky responded honorably in horse language, "You are welcome." He then returned to grazing, following in behind his beloved lead mare.

Creating a sustainable life for the leader creates a sustainable life for the community, and gives agility to its members when they need it the most. Sometimes the most important role of the leader is to rest and trust in her herd.

Epilogue
"And Grace will lead me home." – Lyrics to *Amazing Grace* by John Newton

On June 25, 2007, we signed over the title to Grace Mountain Ranch to its new owners. It was my forty-fourth birthday. Two days later we began our journey across the country. How fitting for this new phase of my life to start on my birthday. I have never given birth to a child of my own and somehow I believe that what I went through over the past six months was the universe's way of giving me my version of the experience. Not only did I have to let go of my attachment to our way of life in Oregon, I actually had to fight several emotional and intellectual battles to get beyond seemingly insurmountable obstacles to get us to North Carolina. It was as if I was being asked the question, Are you sure you are ready to leave the cocoon of Grace Mountain Ranch, and if so, are you ready to fight for possibilities that your new life holds with everything that you have to give? I mentioned earlier that I had a hunch that my faith and the trust and confidence of my herd in my leadership were about to be tested. I was right.

As I loaded my eight trusting horses onto the tractor-trailer horse transport, I made each one of them a promise. "There is nothing for you to be afraid of, we are all together and we are headed home. I will be right behind you. I promise." Prior to our trip, I had had many conversations with them about what was about to happen. As I sat with them, I would visualize the truck they would be on for the trip. In their world, it is a stall that moves. I also visualized us all arriving at Southern Grace together; them greeted by me and led off the trailer by me. And then reality emerged.

During the loading process, I led Dream on first followed by Hope, Lucky, and Galen, all of whom loaded with ease. Then it was time for Yani's herd. Harley was loaded on first to ease Yani's concerns. Harley was as brave and steady as always. Yani was next, and she stated her opinion of this idea very clearly. Her body said to all involved, "Umm, no, I don't think so."

After a few attempts, I stopped the process and stood quietly with her until she relaxed. I put my hands on each side of her face and eased her head down until we were eye to eye and said, "Yani, whether or not you get on this trailer is not an option, because I am not leaving without you and this place is no longer ours. We have to go."

I then turned to the two gentlemen driving the truck and told them to link arms behind her and push while I walked her forward. Then I said, "Guys, on three, let's do this." With a bit more coaxing, Yani walked in the trailer. I can't begin to tell you just how relieved I was at that moment.

Then came Grace, and she was the most difficult. I expected her to just follow her mom. Not happening. After several gut-wrenching, unsuccessful attempts, Yani's anxiety was peaking, and again I stopped the process to think. Who else was there to save the day? Of course, it was Rocky. As Grace stood there watching, I led Rocky about halfway up the ramp to the trailer and said, "Rocky, wait for the baby. She needs you to help her through this."

As Rocky's knees trembled on the ramp, he came to a complete stop, turned, and looked at Grace. We managed to convince her to put her front feet on the ramp, then we led Rocky a little farther away and soon he was on the trailer, but still in the doorway where Grace could see him. It then took four people to push her from behind while I drew her toward me from the front. We inched her forward until both of her front feet were in the trailer and finally she walked in her stall. It was a grueling process for us all, but it was over and now it was time to move on.

As the truck pulled away, our caravan of vehicles fell in behind including a twenty-six ft. U-Haul van carrying everything we owned, followed by my pick-up truck towing an RV with eight cats in it, and finally by Beth's car carrying four dogs. We had six drivers, Beth and me, Beth's Mom "B", her sister Katie, my nephew Gunter, and our family friend, Anne Cloe, a.k.a., "Miss Anne". We were quite a sight to behold. Our journey began with a steep climb through the mountains of eastern Oregon. I was driving the truck with the RV and had never towed a vehicle before. In fact, no one in our crew had ever towed a vehicle before. As the elevation of the mountains increased, it became harder and harder to keep up with the trailer carrying the horses. My body, mind, and soul began to fill with fear and anger at the drivers who kept getting farther away.

Meanwhile, we were already exhausted from packing and loading the moving van the day before. Beth and I were particularly weary, because of the hell we went through in selling our house in Oregon and buying the new place in North Carolina. In the past six months of our real estate drama, we had been lied to, manipulated, cheated, misrepresented, and let down by people who were being paid to protect our interest. My threshold of tolerance had been crossed a long time ago and now I was being faced with yet another no-win situation.

I had to deal with the reality that there was no way we were going to be able to keep pace with the horse transport and that I needed to let my family stop for the night and rest. I knew in my heart how hard they were all trying to keep going, because they knew it would break my heart to leave the horses' sides. I knew I had to make it okay for us to stop and take the pressure off of them to keep moving. When I pulled into the parking lot of a hotel, they all looked worried until I said, "It's okay. They have to stop every five hours to feed, water, and let the horses rest. We will sleep here for a few hours and catch up with them tomorrow."

We started again at 4:00 A.M in the morning and continued from Oregon into Idaho. It wasn't long before the RV was being whipped around by the summer Idaho winds. We had to take it very slowly and began to fall farther and farther behind. By the time we reached Wyoming, we were more than twelve hours behind the horses. I began to fall deeper and deeper into despair and could not think my way through what to do. We had to get there before the horses. It was at this low point that I remembered something my sister said, "If you don't need God's help, it probably isn't worth doing." In that moment, I began working through a solution.

We decided to stop for the night in Rawlins, Wyoming around 10:30 P.M. We then agreed to split up so that Beth, "B", Katie, and Miss Anne could drive the vehicles at a pace that felt safe and rest when they needed to rest. I would take the car with my nephew Gunter, and try to catch up with the horses at their layover facility in York, Nebraska, which was 640 miles from Rawlins. At the layover site, the horses would be taken off the truck, given twelve hours to sleep and stretch their legs, and reloaded with a scheduled departure of 11:00 A.M. In order for me to make it, I had to be up by 4:00 A.M. and drive one hundred miles per hour for six hours and forty minutes. While I was driving, one of my clients called me on my cell phone. I explained to her what was going on and being the woman of faith that she is, she wished us, "God Speed." I replied, "You just have no idea, and thank you."

My saint of a sixteen year old nephew agreed to go with me. I couldn't have done it without him. Believe it or not, we made it just as the truck was completing their fueling at the truck stop prior to getting on the highway. When the drivers saw Gunter and me pull in behind them, they were in complete disbelief, because they knew how far we had to come to catch them. We arrived just in time to let the horses hear our voices and kiss them each on the nose. Gunter and I then followed the horses staying less than two car links behind them, straight through from York, Nebraska to Selma, North Carolina. It was about a thirty-six hour drive including our trip from Rawlins to York.

Each time we stopped to water the horses, the drivers would look at the two of us with sheer amazement. At the final stop, one of the drivers came up to me and said, "Whatever it is that you are using to stay awake, I want some of it."

I turned to him and said, "I am not using anything. This is my family and I made them a promise. The only thing I am using is love." He looked at me like I was speaking a foreign language. It was a miracle in every sense of the word.

For thirty hours, Gunter and I stared at one single image as we crossed eight states. It was the image of the back of a horse trailer that had the words written on it, BOB HUBBARD HORSE TRANSPORTATION, INC; 1-800-472-7786. Befitting the occasion, I couldn't help but think of whose windows we were staring into on the back of the trailer. Of course it was Yani and Grace who were side-by-side. We stayed so close to the truck that Gunter and I were using the draft of the trailer to pull us along the highway. With tears streaming down my face as we crossed the border of Tennessee into North Carolina, I kept hearing the words from the song *Amazing Grace* circling through my mind. "And Grace will lead me home."

As we drove in the driveway, my sister and brother-in-law were sitting on the front porch awaiting our arrival. I led each horse off the trailer and placed their lead lines into the hands of one of my family members. Once off the truck, we walked each of the two herds to their new pastures. Grace was last off the truck and we walked the path to our new home together. A few days later Beth, "B", Katie, and Miss Anne all arrived safe and sound. This part of our journey was complete.

Bibliography

Irwin, Chris. *Horses Don't Lie.* New York: Marlowe and Company, 2001.

Gore, Albert. *An Inconvenient Truth.* New York: Rodale, 2006.

Grandin, Temple. *Animals in Translation.* New York: Scribner, 2005.

Kohanov, Linda. *Riding Between the Worlds: Expanding Our Potential Through The Way of the Horse.* Novato, California: New World Library, 2003.

Palmer, Parker J. *Let Your Life Speak: Listening for the Voice of Vocation.* San Francisco: Jossey-Bass, 2000.

Palmer, Parker J. *The Courage to Teach: Exploring the Inner Landscape of a Teacher's Life.* San Francisco: Jossey-Bass, 1998.

Rector, Barbara K. *Adventures in Awareness: Learning with the Help of Horses.* Bloomington, Indiana: Authorhouse, 2005.

Resnick, Carolyn. *Naked Liberty.* Los Olivos, California: Amigo Publications Inc, 2005.

Strozzi, Ariana. *Horse Sense for the Leader Within.* Bloomington, Indiana: Authorhouse, 2004.

Tarrant, John. *Bring Me the Rinoceros: And Other Zen Koans to Bring You Joy.* New York: Harmony Books, 2004.

Kabat-Zinn, Jon. *Coming to Our Senses: Healing Ourselves and The World Through Mindfulness.* New York: Hyperion, 2005.

About the Author

Dr. June Gunter has twenty-one years of experience working as an educator and leadership development consultant. Her mission is to bring horses and people together to discover more effective ways of leading and of creating healthy communities. June holds a Doctor of Education degree in the field of Adult Learning from North Carolina State University. June attributes many of the lessons she learned about being a teacher and a leader to the horses she has loved from childhood through today. She is a Strozzi Ranch Certified Equine-Guided Educator. In 2004, June founded TeachingHorse LLC.

June is one of the co-founders of EGEA (Equine-Guided Education Association). She is a professional educator committed to embodying the highest standards of adult learning. One of her lifelong goals is to contribute to the field of education by developing innovative ways to engage adults in continuous learning. June is also a certified board member on the Commission for Certification of Equine Facilitated Interaction Professionals (CEFIP).

TeachingHorse provides leadership development workshops and individual coaching with horses. Participants in our workshops experience a new model of leadership based on the skills and abilities that lead mares use to lead their herds. Clients include business, community, and family leaders, as well as people who want to improve their relationship with their horses.

Visit the website at TeachingHorse.com. For more information email junegunter@teachinghorse.com

About the Photographer

Beth Hyjek holds an MFA from St. Mary's College of California and BFA from New York University, Tisch School of the Arts. She is the co-founder of TeachingHorse and a writer/photographer who is constantly amazed by the images and stories that horses share with her and the people who participate in the workshops.

Printed in the United States
91948LV00002B